UKULELE

STRUMMIN' ON THE UKE

ISBN 978-1-4803-9136-9

HAL•LEONARD®
CORPORATION
7777 W. BLUEMOUND RD. P.O. BOX 13819 MILWAUKEE, WI 53213

For all works contained herein:
Unauthorized copying, arranging, adapting, recording, Internet posting, public performance,
or other distribution of the printed music in this publication is an infringement of copyright.
Infringers are liable under the law.

Visit Hal Leonard Online at
www.halleonard.com

CONTENTS

Against the Wind

Words and Music by Bob Seger

First note

Verse
Moderate Rock beat

1. It seems like yes - ter - day, ___
2. *See additional lyrics*
3. *Instrumental*

but it was long a - go. ___

Ja - ney was love - ly. She was the queen of my nights, ___

there in the dark - ness with the ra - di - o play-in' low, ___ and

Copyright © 1980 Gear Publishing Co.
All Rights Reserved   Used by Permission

the se - crets that we shared, _____

the moun - tains that we moved, _____

caught _ like a wild-fire out of con - trol _____ till there was

noth - in' left _____ to burn _____ and noth - in' left to prove. _

Pre-Chorus

1. And I re - mem - ber what she _____ said to
2., 3. *See additional lyrics*

me, _____ how she swore _____ that it nev - er would end. _

Outro

Well, I'm old - er now, ___ and still

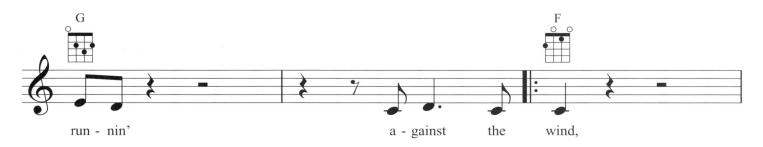

run - nin' a - gainst the wind,

Repeat and fade

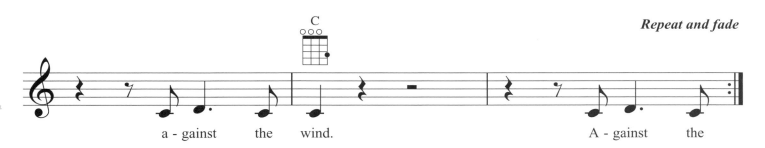

a - gainst the wind. A - gainst the

Additional Lyrics

2. And the years rolled slowly past,
   And I found myself alone,
   Surrounded by strangers I thought were my friends.
   I found myself further and further from my home,
   And I guess I lost my way.
   There were, oh, so many roads.
   I was livin' to run and runnin' to live,
   Never worried about payin', or even how much I owed.

Pre-Chorus: Movin' eight miles a minute for months at a time,
   Breakin' all of the rules that would bend,
   I began to find myself searchin',
   Searchin' for shelter again and again.

Chorus: Against the wind,
   Little somethin' against the wind.
   I found myself seekin' shelter against the wind.

3. *Instrumental*

Pre-Chorus: Well, those drifter's days are past me now.
   I've got so much more to think about:
   Deadlines and commitments,
   What to leave in, what to leave out.

Chorus: Against the wind,
   I'm still runnin' against the wind.
   I'm older now, but still runnin' against the wind.

Baby Blue

Words and Music by Peter Ham

1. Guess I got what I de - serve; kept you wait - ing there too long, my love. with - out a word;
2. All the days be - came so long; did you real - ly think I'd do you wrong? I let you go,
3. Guess that's all I'd have to say, 'cept the feel - ing just grows strong - er ev - 'ry day. be - fore I go:

All that time Dix - ie, when Just one thing

Copyright © 1971 The Estate Of Peter William Ham
Copyright Renewed
All Rights Administered by Kobalt Songs Music Publishing
All Rights Reserved   Used by Permission

F   C   G

did - n't   know ___ you'd think ___   that   I'd   for - get, ___
thought you'd re - al - ize ___   that   I   would know, ___
Take good care, ___ ba - by.   Let me   know, ___

D

or   I'd   re - gret ___
I   would show ___
let   it   grow, ___

Am   C

the spe - cial   love ___   I have for you, ___
the spe - cial   love ___   I have for you, ___
the spe - cial   love ___   you have for me, ___

To Coda θ G

my Ba - by   Blue. ___
my Ba - by   Blue. ___
my Dix - ie   dear. _

Bridge
Bm

What   can   I   do? _
How   can   I   show _

Em   B+

____
______________ you? __________________________

What   can   I   say, _
Show me   a   way. _

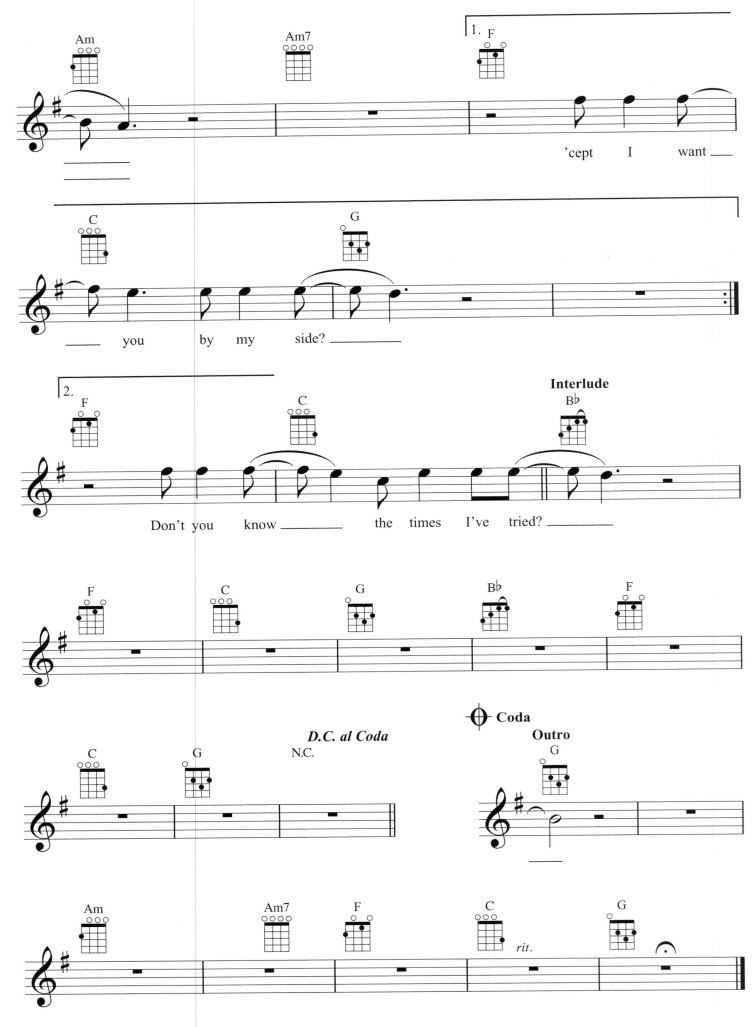

Boulevard of Broken Dreams

Words by Billie Joe
Music by Green Day

First note

Verse
Moderately

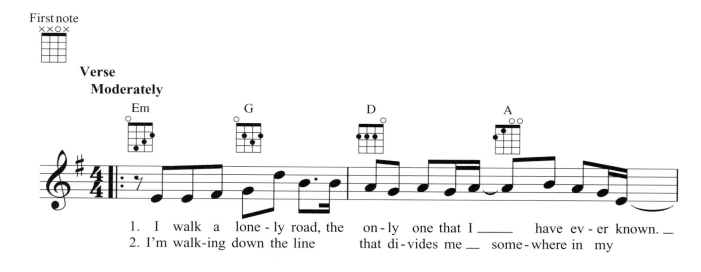

1. I walk a lone - ly road, the on - ly one that I _____ have ev - er known. _
2. I'm walk-ing down the line that di - vides me _ some - where in my

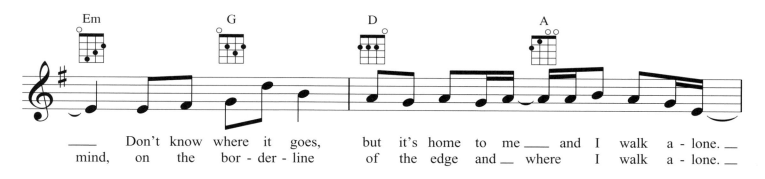

_____ Don't know where it goes, but it's home to me _ and I walk a - lone. _
mind, on the bor - der - line of the edge and _ where I walk a - lone. _

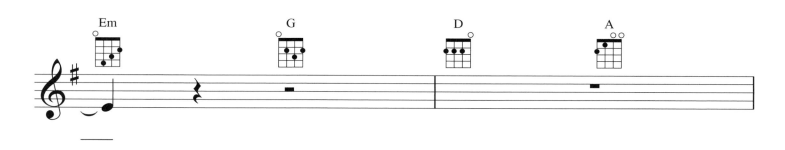

_____

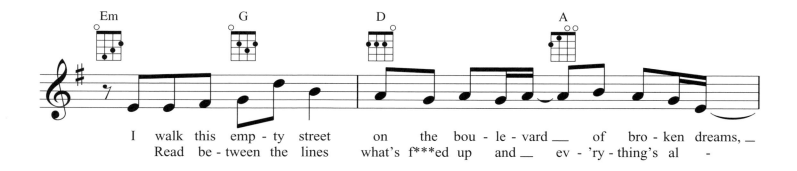

I walk this emp - ty street on the bou - le - vard _ of bro - ken dreams, _
Read be - tween the lines what's f***ed up and _ ev - 'ry - thing's al -

© 2004 WB MUSIC CORP. and GREEN DAZE MUSIC
All Rights Administered by WB MUSIC CORP.
All Rights Reserved   Used by Permission

where the cit - y sleeps, and I'm the on - ly one ⎫ and I walk a - lone.
right. Check my vi - tal signs and know I'm still a - live ⎬

I walk a - lone, I walk a - lone.

I walk a - lone, I walk a...

𝄋 **Chorus**

My shad - ow's the on - ly one that walks be - side me.

My shal - low heart's the on - ly thing that's beat - ing.

Some - times I wish some - one out there will find me.

12

Baby Can I Hold You

Words and Music by Tracy Chapman

© 1988 EMI APRIL MUSIC INC. and PURPLE RABBIT MUSIC
All Rights Controlled and Administered by EMI APRIL MUSIC INC.
All Rights Reserved   International Copyright Secured   Used by Permission

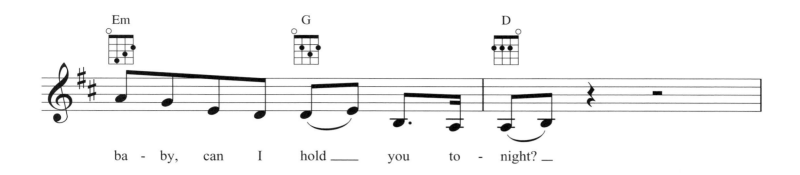

ba - by, can I hold ____ you to - night? ____

May - be if I told ____ you the right words, ooh, ____ at the right ____

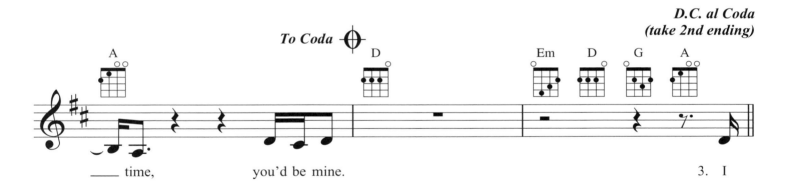

D.C. al Coda
(take 2nd ending)

To Coda

____ time, you'd be mine. 3. I

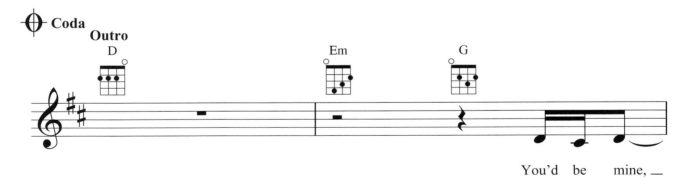

Coda
Outro

You'd be mine, ____

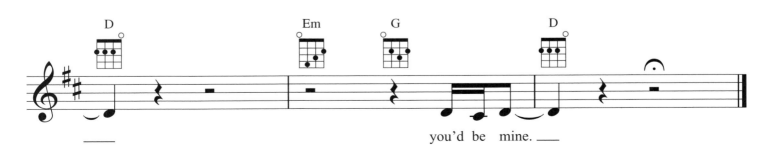

____ you'd be mine. ____

Baby, I Love Your Way

Words and Music by Peter Frampton

Copyright © 1975 ALMO MUSIC CORP. and NUAGES ARTISTS MUSIC LTD.
Copyright Renewed
All Rights Controlled and Administered by ALMO MUSIC CORP.
All Rights Reserved   Used by Permission

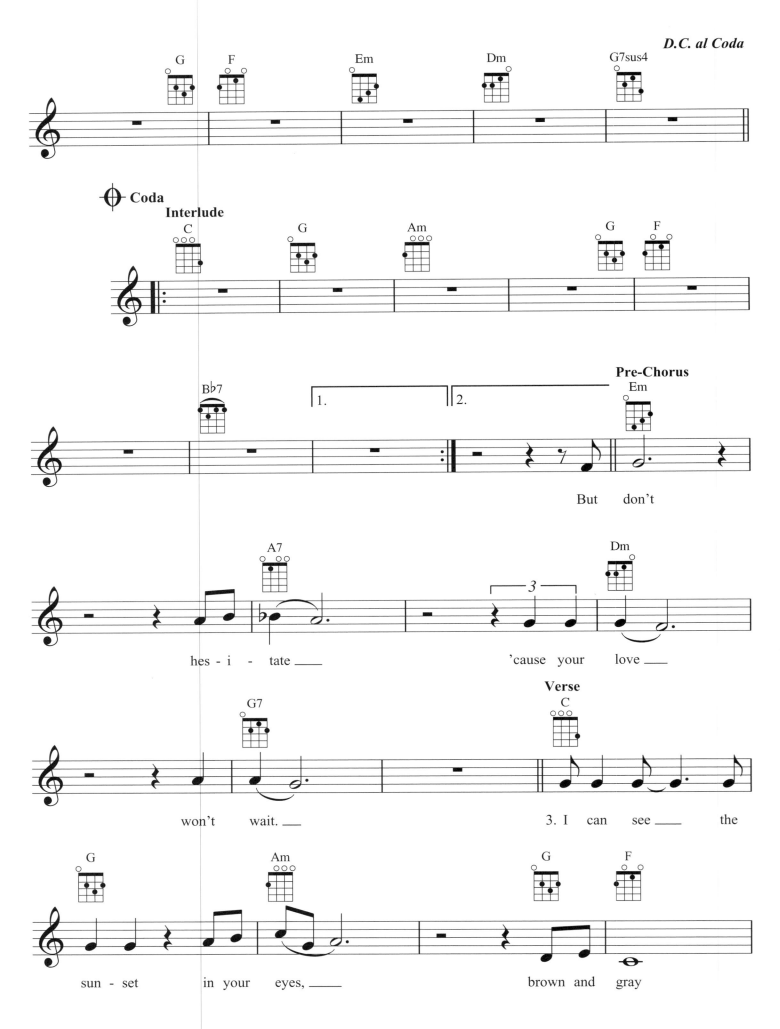

and   blue   be - sides.   Clouds are stalk - ing

is - lands   in   the   sun. ____   I wish I could

buy   one   out of sea - son.   But

Pre-Chorus

don't   hes - i - tate ____   'cause your

love _____   won't   wait. _____

Outro-Chorus   *Repeat and fade*

Ooh,   ba - by, I love ___ your way. _____
Wan - na   tell you I love ___ your way. _____
Wan - na   be with you night ___ and day. _____

Back Home Again

Words and Music by John Denver

Copyright © 1974; Renewed 2002 Anna Kate Deutschendorf, Zachary Deutschendorf and Jesse Belle Denver in the U.S.
All Rights for Anna Kate Deutschendorf and Zachary Deutschendorf Administered by BMG Rights Management (US) LLC
All Rights for Jesse Belle Denver Administered by WB Music Corp.
International Copyright Secured   All Rights Reserved

To Coda ⊕

C

_____ that makes him warm. _____
_____ just yes - ter - day. _____
_____ that makes me

Chorus

F   G7   C

Hey, it's good to be back home _____ a - gain. _____

F   G7

_____ Some - times _____ this old farm _____ feels _____

C   F   G7

_____ like a long - lost friend. Yes, and hey, it's good _____ to

C

1.

be back home a - gain. _____   3. There's

2.   **Bridge**

C7   F   G7

And, oh, the time that I can lay _____ this tired _____

old bod - y down   and feel your fin - gers

feath - er soft up - on me, _____ the

kiss - es _____ that I live for,   the love that lights my way, _

_____   the hap - pi - ness _____   that

liv - in' with you brings me. _____   4. It's the

Coda

warm. _____

Barely Breathing

Words and Music by Duncan Sheik

Copyright © 1996 by Universal Music - Careers, Duncan Sheik Songs and Happ-Dog Music
All Rights Administered by Universal Music - Careers
International Copyright Secured   All Rights Reserved

good - bye. _____ 'Cause I am bare - ly

𝄋𝄋 **Chorus**

breath - ing, and I can't find the air. Don't know who I'm

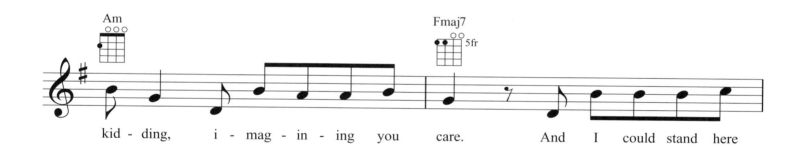

kid - ding, i - mag - in - ing you care. And I could stand here

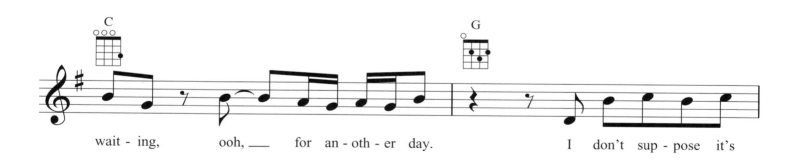

wait - ing, ooh, ___ for an - oth - er day. I don't sup - pose it's

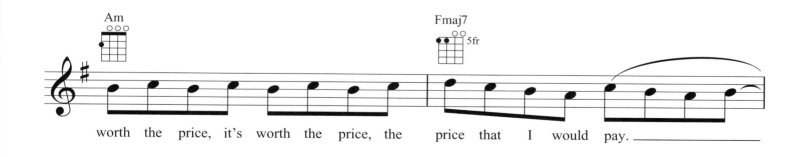

worth the price, it's worth the price, the price that I would pay. _____

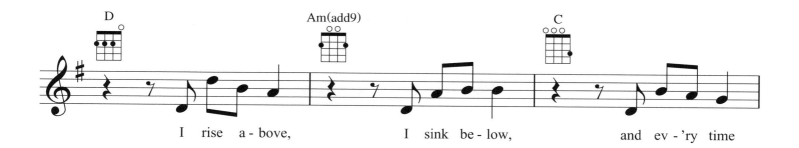

I rise a-bove, I sink be-low, and ev-'ry time

you come and go. ___ Please don't come ___ and go. ___

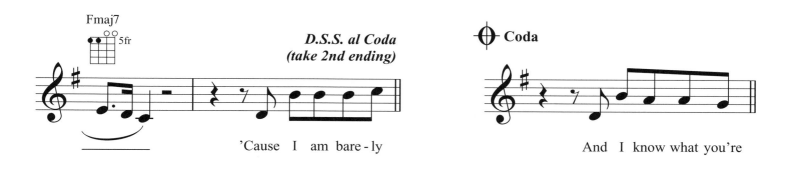

D.S.S. al Coda
(take 2nd ending)

⊕ **Coda**

___ 'Cause I am bare-ly

And I know what you're

Outro

do-ing. I see it all _____ too clear.

Additional Lyrics

2. I believed in your confusion, so completely torn.
   It must have been that yesterday was the day that I was born.
   There's not much to examine, nothing left to hide.
   You really can't be serious; you have to ask me why I say goodbye.

3. And ev'ryone keeps asking: What's it all about?
   It used to be so certain; now I can't figure out.
   What is this attraction? I only feel the pain.
   And nothing left to reason, and only you to blame. Will it ever change?

Building a Mystery

Words and Music by Sarah McLachlan and Pierre Marchand

Copyright © 1997 Sony/ATV Music Publishing LLC, Tyde Music and Pierre J. Marchand
All Rights on behalf of Sony/ATV Music Publishing LLC and Tyde Music Administered by
Sony/ATV Music Publishing LLC, 424 Church Street, Suite 1200, Nashville, TN 37219
International Copyright Secured   All Rights Reserved

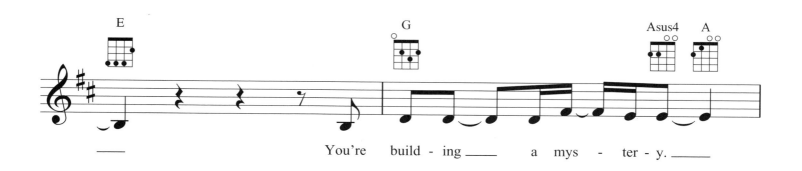

You're build-ing ____ a mys - ter-y. ____

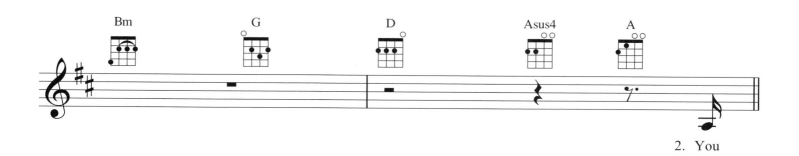

2. You

Verse

live in a church where you sleep __ with voo - doo ____ dolls, _____ and you
(3.) scream-ing a - loud a prayer __ from your se - cret god. __ You

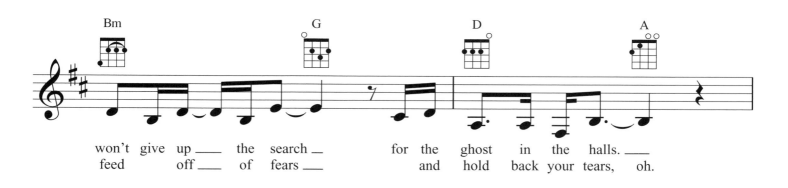

won't give up ____ the search __ for the ghost in the halls. ____
feed off ____ of fears ____ and hold back your tears, oh.

You wear san - dals in ____ the snow __ and a _____ smile that won't wash __ a - way.
You give us a tan - trum __ and a _____ know - it - all ____ grin, __

Can you look out the win-dow with-out your __ shad-ow get-ting in __ the way? __
just when you need one when the __ eve-ning's thin.

Pre-Chorus

You're __ so beau-ti - ful, __ with an edge and charm - ing.
You're __ a beau-ti - ful, __ a beau-ti-ful, f**ked-up man.

You're so care - ful when I'm in your arms. __
You set it up, your ra - zor - wire __ shrine. __

Chorus

__ 'Cause you're work - ing,
__ 'Cause you're work - ing,
(D.S.) __ Yeah, you're work - ing,
build - ing __ a mys - ter - y, __

__ hold - ing on __ and hold - ing it __ in.

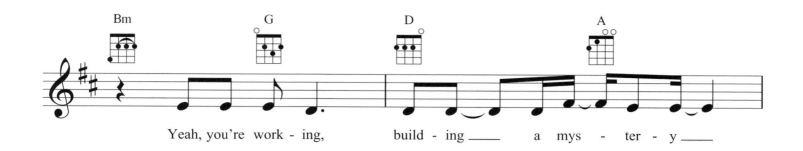

Yeah, you're work - ing, build - ing ____ a mys - ter - y ____

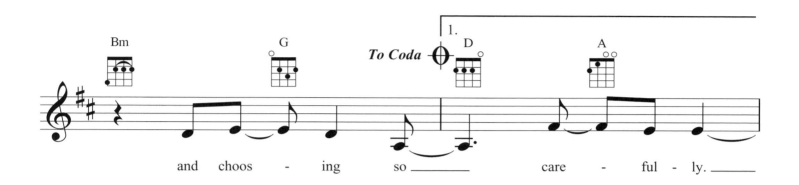

and choos - ing so ____ care - ful - ly. ____

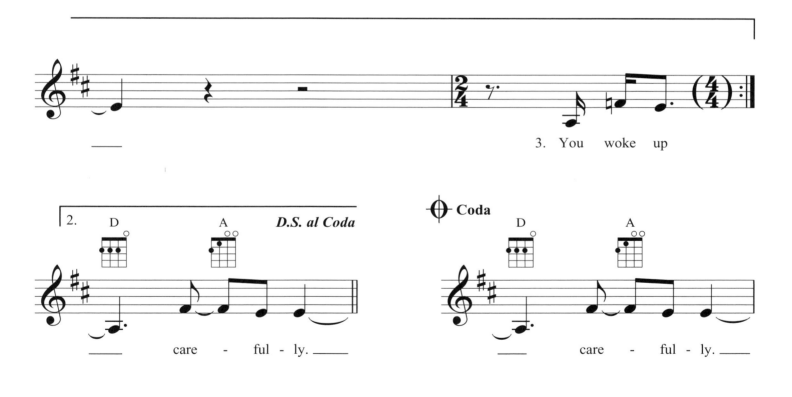

____ 3. You woke up

D.S. al Coda — 2. D A

____ care - ful - ly. ____

Coda — D A

____ care - ful - ly. ____

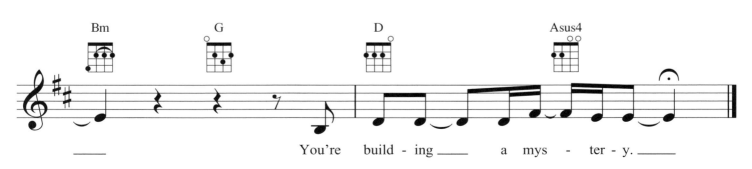

____ You're build - ing ____ a mys - ter - y. ____

Catch the Wind

Words and Music by Donovan Leitch

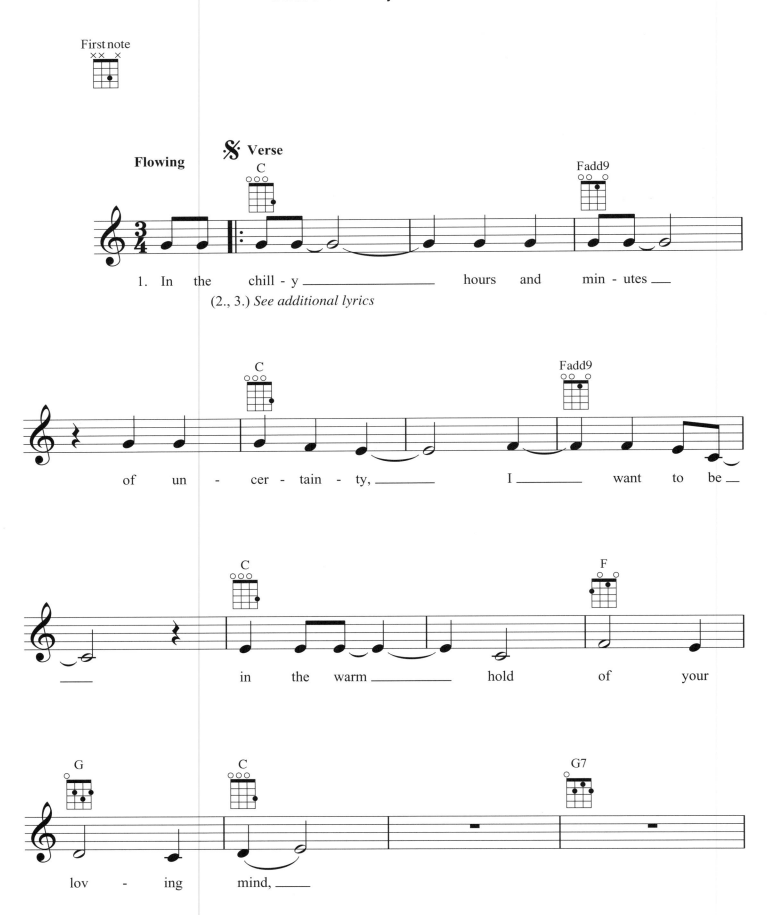

Copyright © 1965 by Donovan (Music) Ltd.
Copyright Renewed
All Rights Administered by Southern Music Publishing Co. Inc.
International Copyright Secured   All Rights Reserved

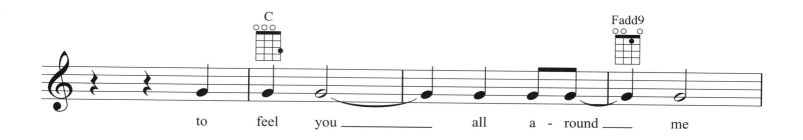

to feel you _____ all a - round ____ me

and to take ____ your hand _____ a - long the sand. __

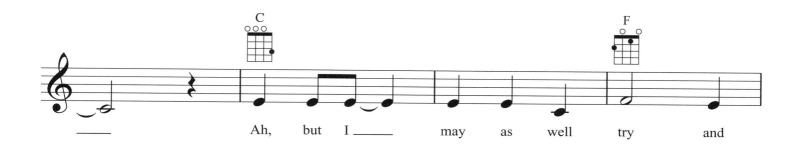

____ Ah, but I _____ may as well try and

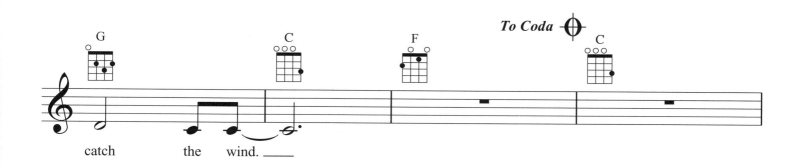

To Coda ⊕

catch the wind. ____

1. | | 2. | **Interlude**

2. When

Dee dee dee dee _____ dee dee

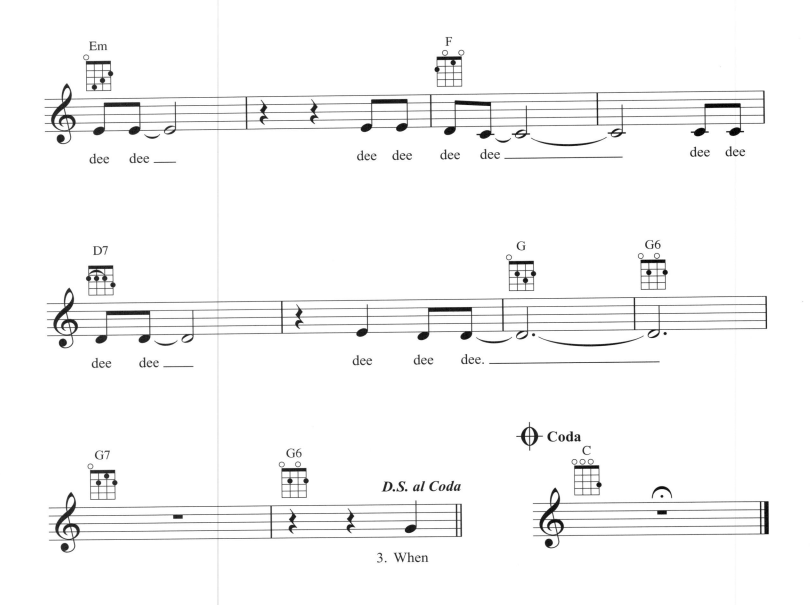

D.S. al Coda

3. When

Additional Lyrics

2. When sundown pales the sky,
   I want to hide a while behind your smile,
   And everywhere I'd look, your eyes I'd find.
   For me to love you now would be the sweetest thing;
   'Twould make me sing.
   Ah, but I may as well try and catch the wind.

3. When rain has hung the leaves with tears,
   I want you near to kill my fears,
   To help me to leave all my blues behind.
   For standing in your heart is where I want to be
   And long to be.
   Ah, but I may as well try and catch the wind.

Breaking the Girl

Words and Music by Anthony Kiedis, Flea, John Frusciante and Chad Smith

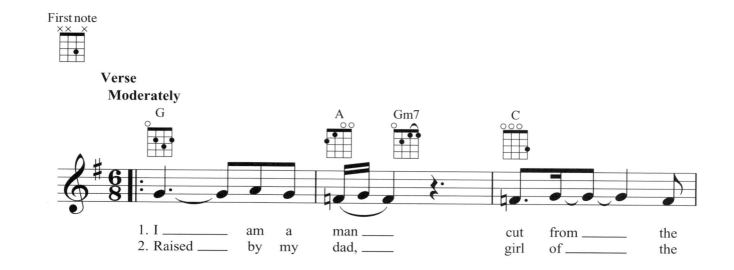

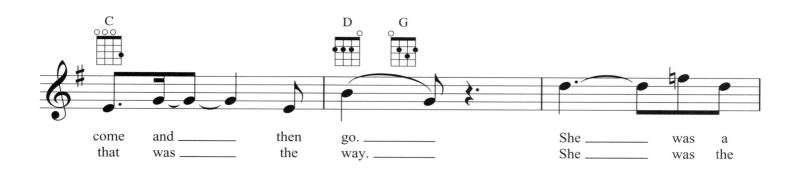

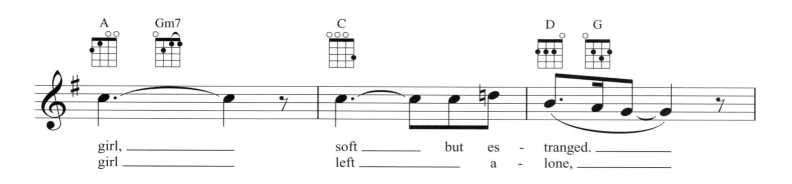

© 1991 MOEBETOBLAME MUSIC
All Rights Reserved   Used by Permission

Pre-Chorus

Chorus

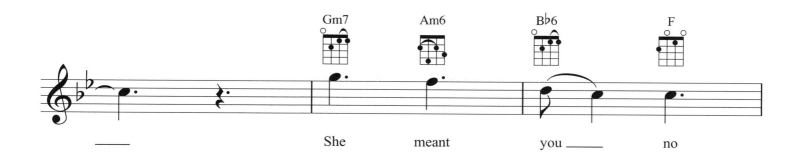

She meant you ____ no

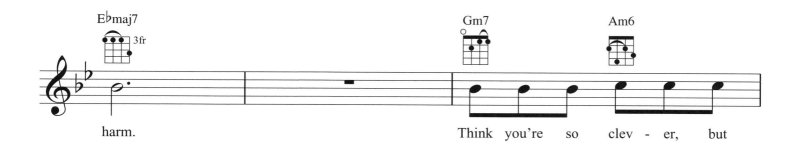

harm. Think you're so clev - er, but

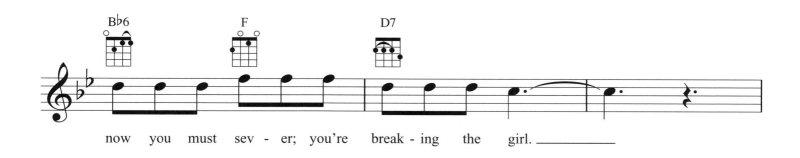

now you must sev - er; you're break - ing the girl. _____

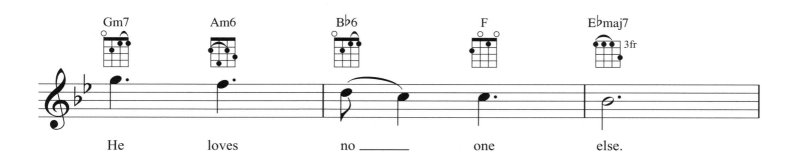

He loves no ____ one else.

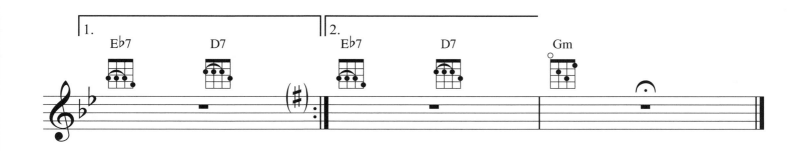

Closer to Fine

Words and Music by Emily Saliers and Amy Ray

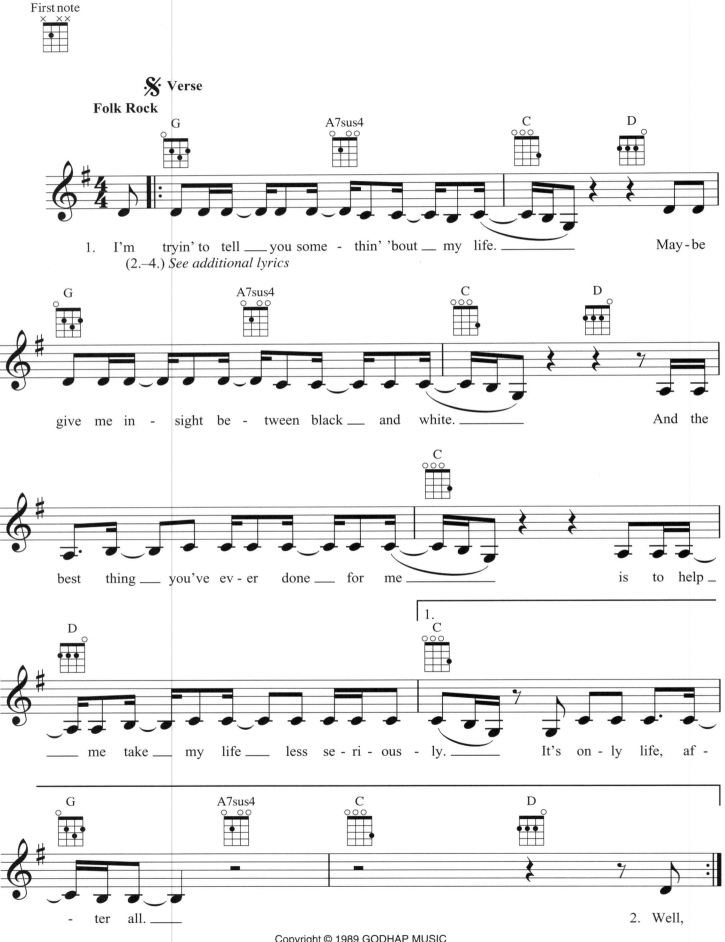

Copyright © 1989 GODHAP MUSIC
All Rights Controlled and Administered by SONGS OF UNIVERSAL, INC.
All Rights Reserved   Used by Permission

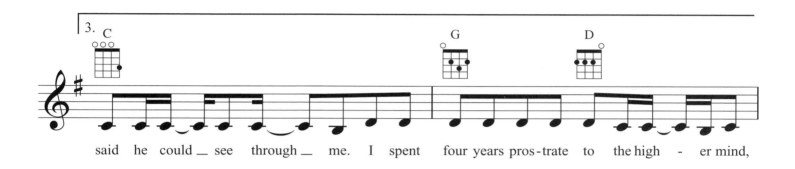

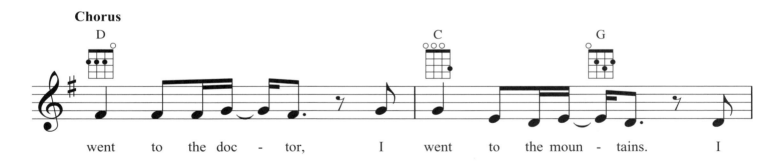

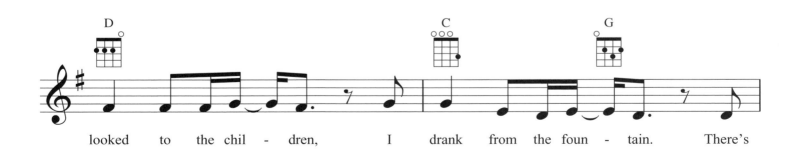

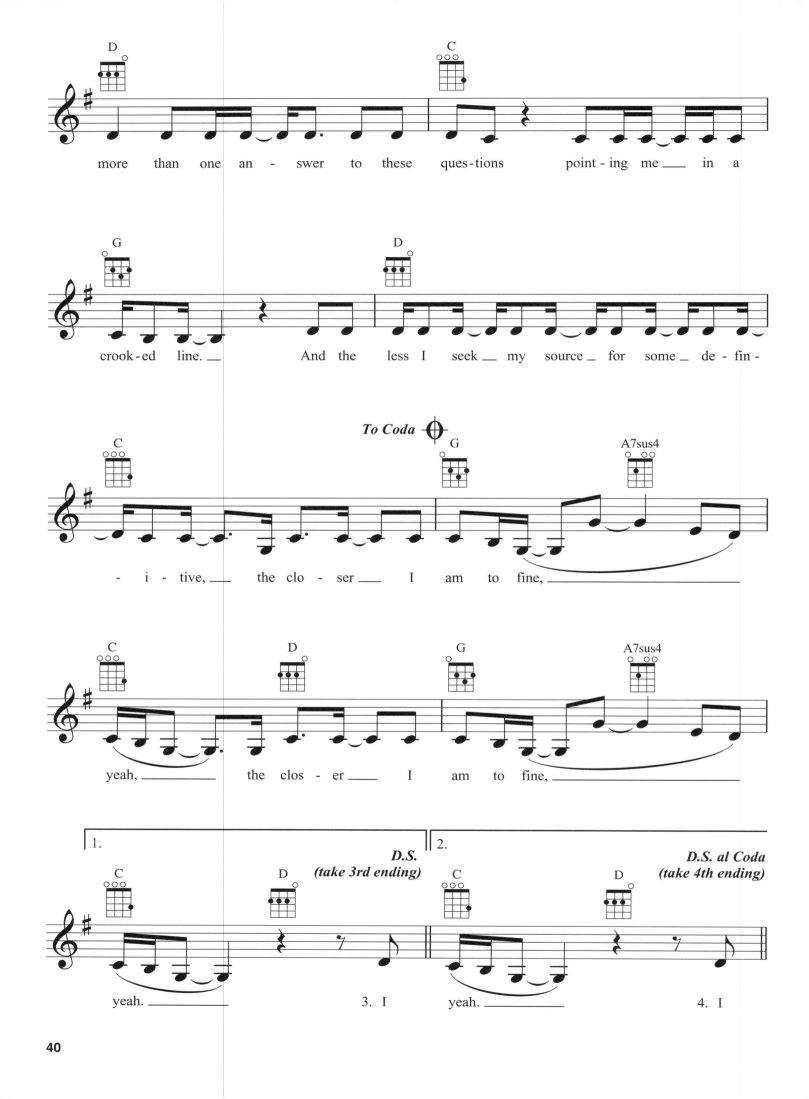

more than one an - swer to these ques-tions point - ing me ___ in a

crook - ed line. ___ And the less I seek ___ my source ___ for some ___ de - fin -

- i - tive, ___ the clo - ser ___ I am to fine,

yeah, ___ the clos - er ___ I am to fine,

1.

D.S.
(take 3rd ending)

yeah. ___

3. I

2.

D.S. al Coda
(take 4th ending)

yeah. ___

4. I

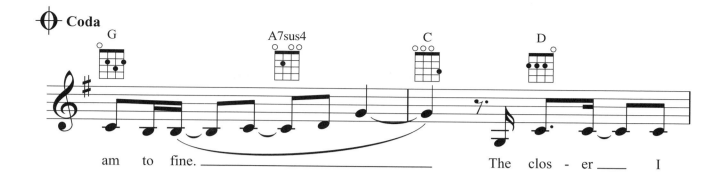

Coda

am   to   fine. _____ The clos - er ____ I

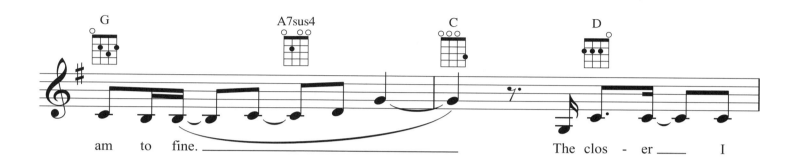

am   to   fine. _____ The clos - er ____ I

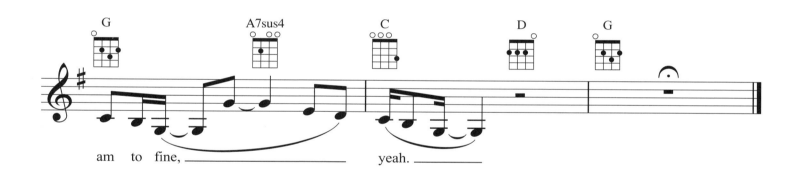

am   to   fine, _____ yeah. _____

Additional Lyrics

2. Well, darkness has a hunger that's insatiable, and lightness has a call that's hard to hear.
   I wrap my fear around me like a blanket.
   I sailed my ship of safety till I sank it.
   I'm crawling on your shores.

3. I went to the Doctor of Philosophy with a poster of Rasputin and a beard down to his knee.
   He never did marry or see a B-grade movie.
   He graded my performance, he said he could see through me.
   I spent four years prostate to the higher mind, got my paper and I was free.

4. I stopped by a bar at 3 A.M. to seek solace in a bottle, or possibly a friend.
   I woke up with a headache like my head against a board,
   Twice as cloudy as I'd been the night before.
   And I went in seeking clarity.

Copperhead Road

Words and Music by Steve Earle

© 1988 WB MUSIC CORP., DUKE OF EARLE MUSIC and WARNER-OLIVE MUSIC LLC
All Rights for DUKE OF EARLE MUSIC Administered by WB MUSIC CORP.
All Rights for WARNER-OLIVE MUSIC LLC Administered by UNIVERSAL MUSIC CORP. (Publishing) and ALFRED MUSIC (Print)
All Rights Reserved   Used by Permission

He'd buy a hun-dred pounds of yeast and some

cop - per line.

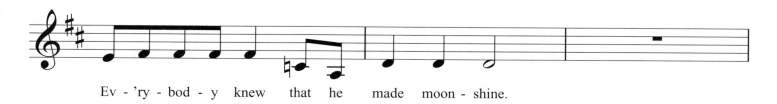

Ev - 'ry - bod - y knew that he made moon - shine.

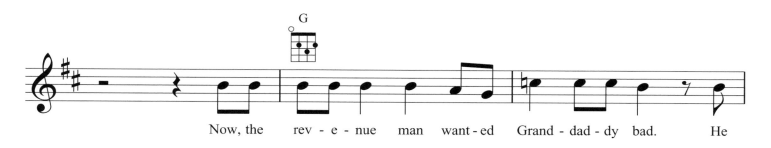

Now, the rev - e - nue man want - ed Grand - dad - dy bad. He

head - ed up a hol - ler with ev - 'ry - thing he had. __ Be - fore my time, __ but I've __

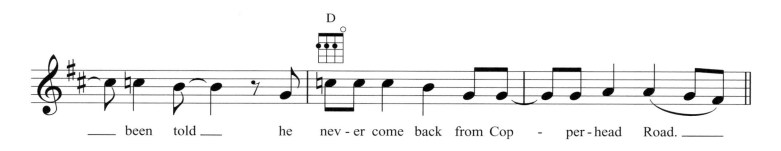

__ been told __ he nev - er come back from Cop - per - head Road. _____

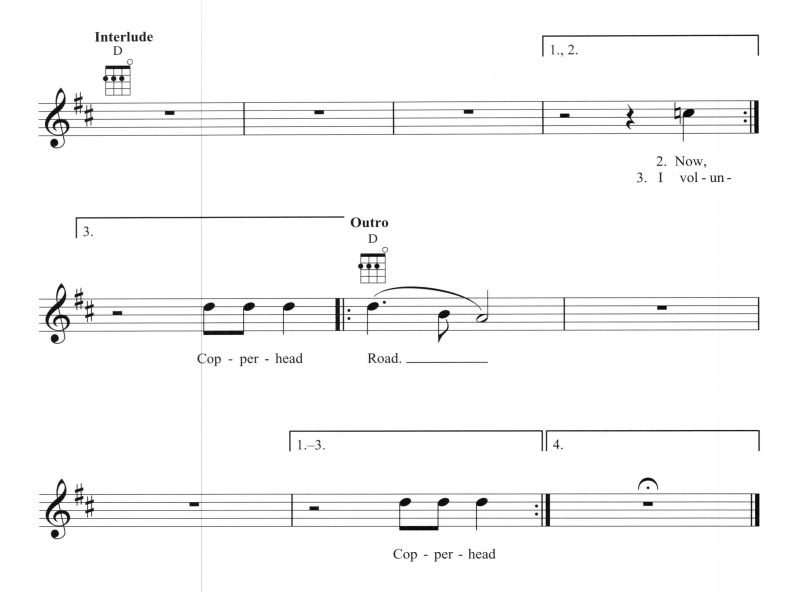

2. Now,
3. I vol - un -

Cop - per - head   Road. _____

Cop - per - head

Additional Lyrics

2. Now, Daddy ran the whiskey in a big-block Dodge.
   Bought it at an auction at the Mason's Lodge.
   "Johnson County Sheriff" painted on the side.
   Just shot a coat of primer, then he looked inside.
   Well, him and my uncle tore that engine down.
   I still remember that rumblin' sound.
   Then the sheriff came around in the middle of the night.
   I heard Mama cryin'; knew somethin' wasn't right.
   He was headed down to Knoxville with the weekly load.
   You could smell the whiskey burnin' down Copperhead Road.

3. I volunteered for the Army on my birthday.
   They draft the white trash first 'round here anyway.
   I done two tours of duty in Vietnam.
   I came home with a brand-new plan.
   I'd take the seed from Colombia and Mexico.
   I'd just plant it up a holler down Copperhead Road.
   Now the DEA's got a chopper in the air.
   I wake up screamin' like I'm back over there.
   I learned a thing or two from Charlie, don't you know.
   You better stay away from Copperhead Road.

Constant Craving

Words and Music by k.d. lang and Ben Mink

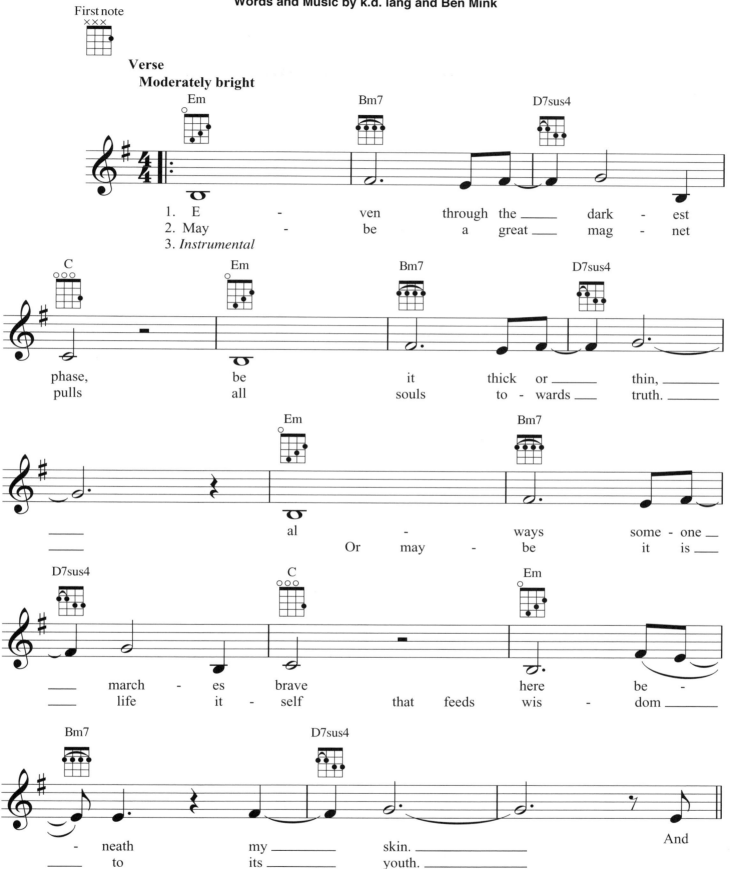

Copyright © 1992 UNIVERSAL - POLYGRAM INTERNATIONAL PUBLISHING, INC.,
BUMSTEAD PRODUCTIONS U.S., INC., ALMO MUSIC CORP. and ZAVION ENTERPRISES, INC.
All Rights for BUMSTEAD PRODUCTIONS U.S., INC. Controlled and Administered by
UNIVERSAL - POLYGRAM INTERNATIONAL PUBLISHING, INC.
All Rights for ZAVION ENTERPRISES, INC. in the world outside the U.S. and Canada
Controlled and Administered by ALMO MUSIC CORP.
All Rights Reserved   Used by Permission

ways ___ been.

D.C. al Coda

⊕ **Coda**

Outro-Chorus

Con - stant crav - ing has

al - ways been.

Crav - ing. Ah,

ha, ___ con - stant crav - ing has

Repeat and fade

al - ways ___ been. ___ Has

Crazy Little Thing Called Love

Words and Music by Freddie Mercury

1. Oh, this thing _____ (4.) called love, well, I just _____

(2., 3.) *See additional lyrics*

_____ can't _____ han - dle it. _____ This thing _____ called

love, I _____ must _____ get a - round to it. _____ I ain't _____

read - y. Cra - zy lit - tle thing called

love.

1., 3. | **2.**

2. Well, this thing _ There goes my
4. This thing _

© 1979 QUEEN MUSIC LTD.
All Rights for the U.S. and Canada Controlled and Administered by BEECHWOOD MUSIC CORP.
All Rights for the world excluding the U.S. and Canada Controlled and Administered by EMI MUSIC PUBLISHING LTD.
All Rights Reserved   International Copyright Secured   Used by Permission

Bridge

Additional Lyrics

2. Well, this thing called love, it cries in a cradle all night.
   It swings, it jives, it shakes all over like a jellyfish. I kinda like it.
   Crazy little thing called love.

3. I gotta be cool, relax, get hip, get on my tracks.
   Take a back seat, hitchhike and take a long ride on a motorbike until I'm ready.
   Crazy little thing called love.

Drift Away

Words and Music by Mentor Williams

Copyright © 1972 ALMO MUSIC CORP.
Copyright Renewed
All Rights Reserved   Used by Permission

Chorus

Oh, give me the beat, __ boys, and free my soul. __ I

wan - na get lost in your rock and roll __ and drift a - way. __

Oh, give me the beat, __ boys, and free my soul. __ I

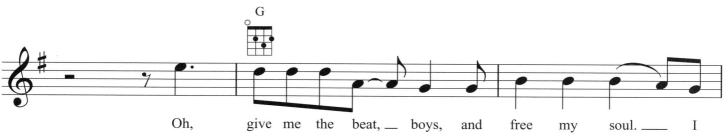

wan - na get lost in your rock and roll __ and drift a - way. __

To Coda ⊕

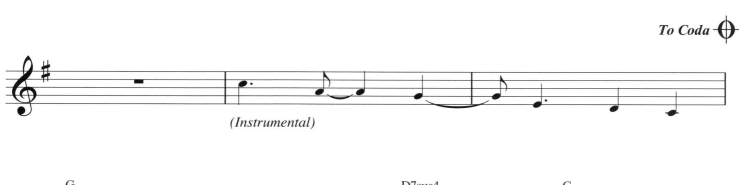

(Instrumental)

Bridge

And when my mind _____ is free, _____

you know a mel - o - dy can move _____ me.

And when I'm feel - in' blue, _____

the gui - tar's com - in' through _ to

D.C. al Coda

⊕ Coda

soothe me. _____

Additional Lyrics

2. Beginnin' to think that I'm wastin' time.
   I don't understand the things I do.
   The world outside looks so unkind,
   And I'm countin' on you to carry me through.

3. Thanks for the joy that you've given me.
   I want you to know I believe in your song
   And rhythm and rhyme and harmony.
   You help me along, makin' me strong.

Daughter

Words and Music by Stone Gossard, Jeffrey Ament,
Eddie Vedder, Michael McCready and David Abbruzzese

First note

Verse
Moderately

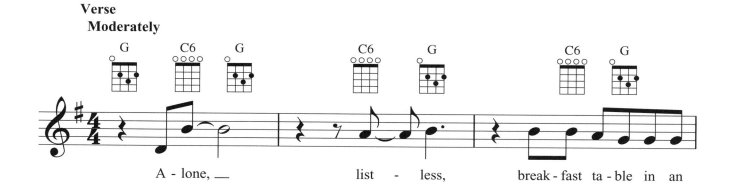

A - lone, ____ list - less, break - fast ta - ble in an

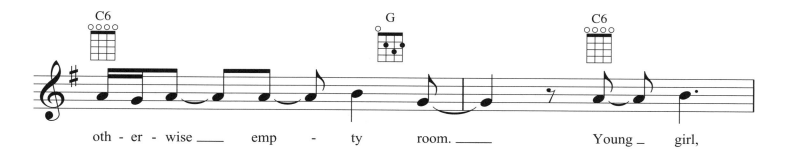

oth - er - wise ____ emp - ty room. ____ Young _ girl,

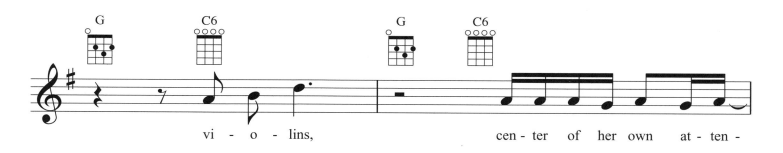

vi - o - lins, cen - ter of her own at - ten -

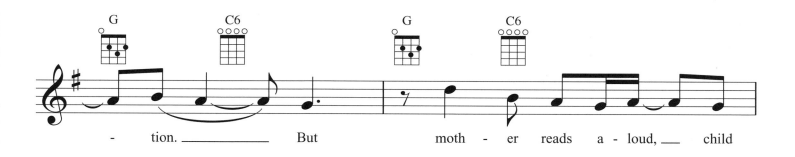

- tion. _____ But moth - er reads a - loud, __ child

Copyright © 1993 UNIVERSAL - POLYGRAM INTERNATIONAL PUBLISHING, INC., WRITE TREATAGE MUSIC,
SCRIBING C-MENT SONGS, INNOCENT BYSTANDER MUSIC, JUMPIN' CAT MUSIC and PICKLED FISH MUSIC
All Rights for WRITE TREATAGE MUSIC and SCRIBING C-MENT SONGS Controlled and Administered by
UNIVERSAL - POLYGRAM INTERNATIONAL PUBLISHING, INC.
All Rights Reserved   Used by Permission

not fit ____ to. The pic - ture kept ____

____ will re - mind _____ me. Don't call ____ me.

Bridge

She holds ____ the hand _____ that holds ____ her down. _

____ She will rise ____ a - bove. ____

Interlude

Coda

Outro

The shades ____ go down. _____

55

Every Rose Has Its Thorn

Words and Music by Bobby Dall, C.C. Deville, Bret Michaels and Rikki Rockett

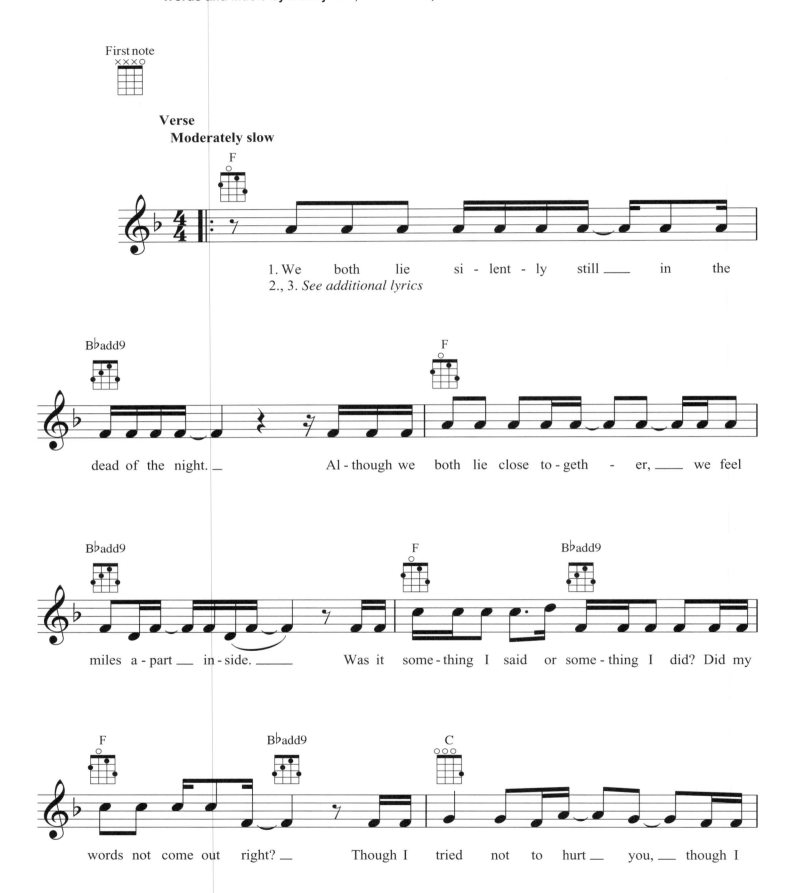

Copyright © 1988 by Cyanide Publishing
All Rights in the United States Administered by Universal Music - Z Songs
International Copyright Secured   All Rights Reserved

tried,   but I guess that's   why ___ they say   ev - 'ry rose ___ has its

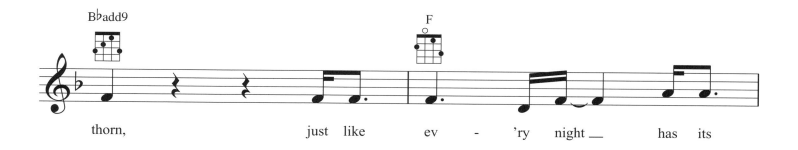

thorn,   just like   ev - 'ry night ___ has its

dawn. ___   Just like   ev - 'ry cow - boy ___ sings his

sad,   sad ___ song,   ev - 'ry rose ___ has its thorn.   2. I

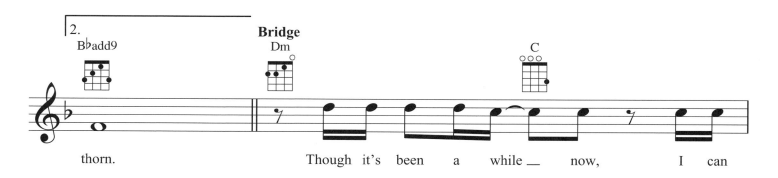

thorn.   Though it's been a while ___ now,   I can

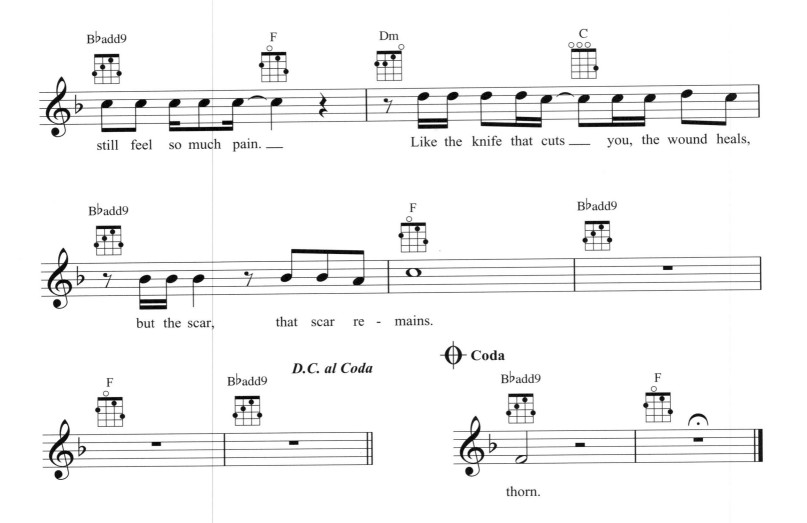

still feel so much pain. — Like the knife that cuts ___ you, the wound heals,

but the scar, that scar re - mains.

D.C. al Coda

Coda

thorn.

Additional Lyrics

2. I listen to our favorite song playing on the radio,
   Hear the DJ say love's a game of easy come and easy go.
   But I wonder, does he know? Has he ever felt like this?
   And I know that you'd be here right now if I could've let you know somehow.
   I guess... *(To Chorus)*

3. I know I could have saved our love that night if I'd known what to say.
   Instead of making love, we both made our separate ways.
   And now I hear you've found somebody new and that I never meant that much to you.
   To hear that tears me up inside and to see you cuts me like a knife.
   I guess... *(To Chorus)*

Ho Hey

Words and Music by Jeremy Fraites and Wesley Schultz

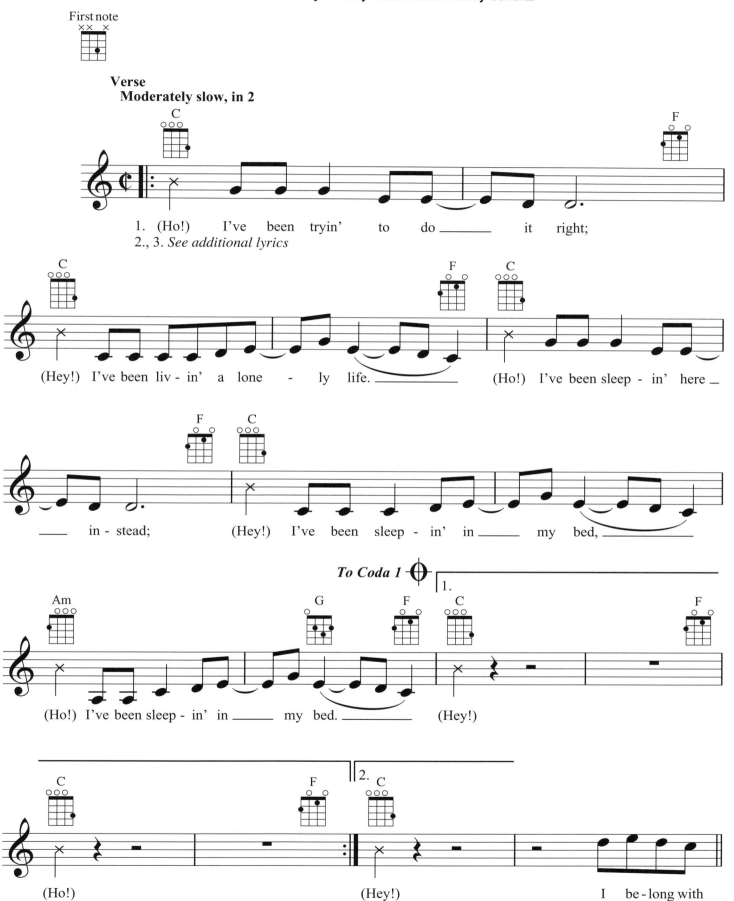

Copyright © 2011 The Lumineers
All Rights Exclusively Administered by Songs Of Kobalt Music Publishing
All Rights Reserved   Used by Permission

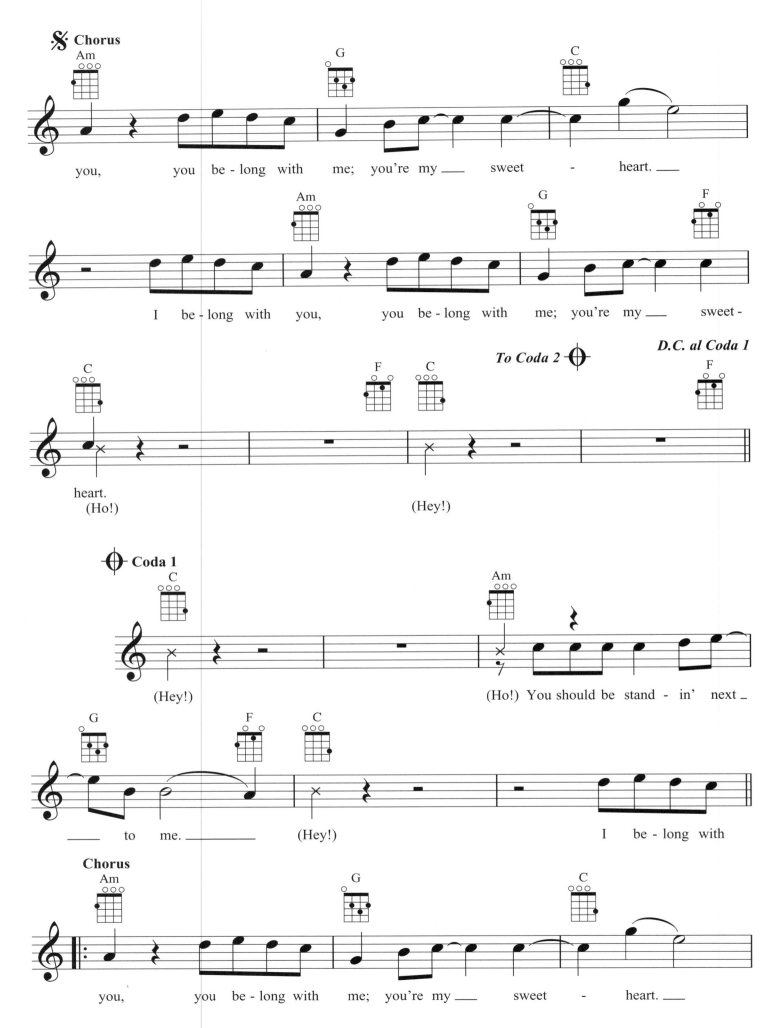

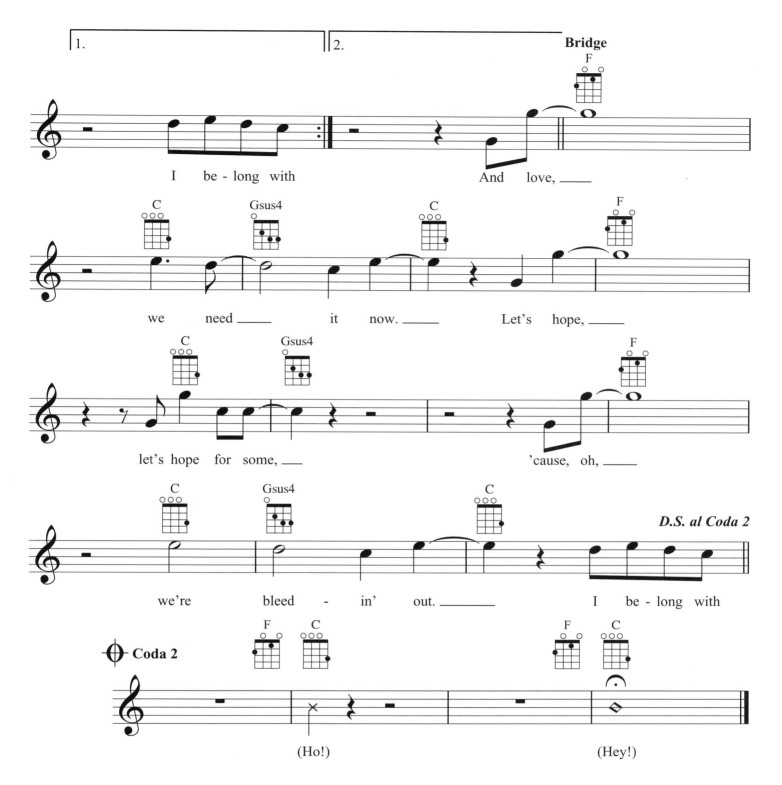

(Ho!)   (Hey!)

Additional Lyrics

2. (Ho!) So show me, family,
   (Hey!) All the blood that I will bleed.
   (Ho!) I don't know where I belong,
   (Hey!) I don't know where I went wrong,
   (Ho!) But I can write a song.
   (Hey!)

3. (Ho!) I don't think you're right for him.
   (Hey!) Look at what it might have been if you
   (Ho!) Took a bus to Chinatown.
   (Hey!) I'd be standing on Canal
   (Ho!) And Bowery. *(To Coda 1)*

Hey, Soul Sister

Words and Music by Pat Monahan, Espen Lind and Amund Bjorkland

© 2009 EMI APRIL MUSIC INC., BLUE LAMP MUSIC and STELLAR SONGS LTD.
All Rights for BLUE LAMP MUSIC Controlled and Administered by EMI APRIL MUSIC INC.
All Rights for STELLAR SONGS LTD. in the U.S. and Canada Controlled and Administered by EMI BLACKWOOD MUSIC INC.
All Rights Reserved   International Copyright Secured   Used by Permission

Additional Lyrics

2. Just in time, I'm so glad you have a one-track mind like me.
    You gave my life direction,
    A game-show love connection we can't deny.
    I'm so obsessed, my heart is bound to beat right out my un-trimmed chest.
    I believe in you. Like a virgin, you're Madonna
    And I'm always gonna wanna blow your mind.

Hickory Wind

Words and Music by Gram Parsons and Bob Buchanan

© 1969 (Renewed 1997) GPJ MUSIC (BMI), HOT BURRITO MUSIC (BMI)/Administered by BUG MUSIC, INC., A BMG CHRYSALIS COMPANY,
STATE ONE MUSIC AMERICA (BMI) and SIXTEEN STARS MUSIC (BMI)
All Rights Reserved Used by Permission

I al - ways pre - tend
each time it be - gins
each time it be - gins

that I'm get - ting the feel
call - ing me home,
call - ing me home,

of hick - o - ry wind.
hick - o - ry wind.
hick - o - ry wind.

1., 2.

3.

2. I start - ed out
3. It's a hard way to

Keeps

Outro

call - ing me home, _____

hick - o - ry wind.

Homeward Bound

Words and Music by Paul Simon

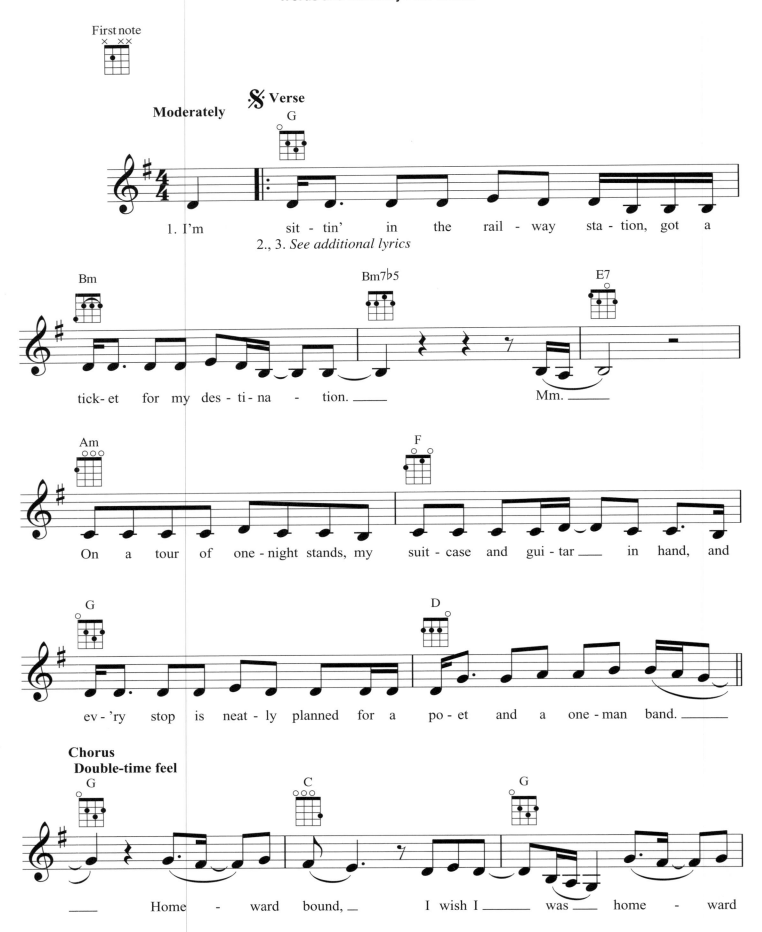

Copyright © 1966 Paul Simon (BMI)
International Copyright Secured   All Rights Reserved
Used by Permission

bound. _____ Home, where my thought's _ es - cap - in'.

End double-time feel

Home, where my mu - sic's play - in'. Home, where my love __ lies wait - ing

To Coda ⊕

D.S. al Coda

si - lent - ly for _____ me. _____ me. _____ 3. To -

⊕ **Coda**

_____ me, si - lent - ly for _____ me.

Outro

(Instrumental)

Additional Lyrics

2. Ev'ry day's an endless stream of cigarettes and magazines. Mm.
   And each town looks the same to me, the movies and the factories,
   And ev'ry stranger's face I see reminds me that I long to be...

3. Tonight I'll sing my songs again, I'll play the game and pretend. Mm.
   But all my words come back to me in shades of mediocrity.
   Like emptiness and harmony, I need someone to comfort me.

A Horse with No Name

Words and Music by Dewey Bunnell

© 1972 (Renewed) WARNER/CHAPPELL MUSIC LTD.
All Rights for the Western Hemisphere Controlled by WB MUSIC CORP.
All Rights Reserved   Used by Permission

Additional Lyrics

2. After two days in the desert sun, my skin began to turn red.
   After three days in the desert fun, I was looking at a river bed.
   And the story it told of a river that flowed made me sad to think it was dead.
   (Skip to Chorus)

3. After nine days, I let the horse run free 'cause the desert had turned to sea.
   There were plants and birds and rocks and things, there were sand and hills and rings.
   The ocean is a desert with its life underground and the perfect disguise above.
   Under the cities lies a heart made of ground, but the humans will give no love.

Hold You in My Arms

Words and Music by Ray LaMontagne and Ethan Johns

Copyright © 2004 BMG Monarch, Sweet Mary Music, BMG Blue and Three Crows Music
All Rights Administered by BMG Rights Management (US) LLC
All Rights Reserved   Used by Permission

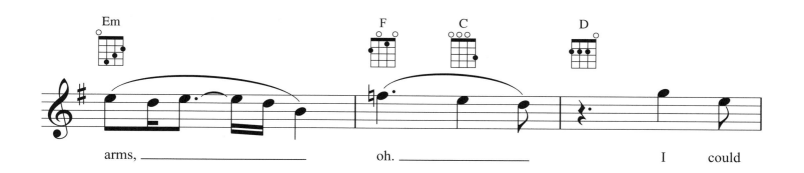

arms, _____ oh. _____ I could

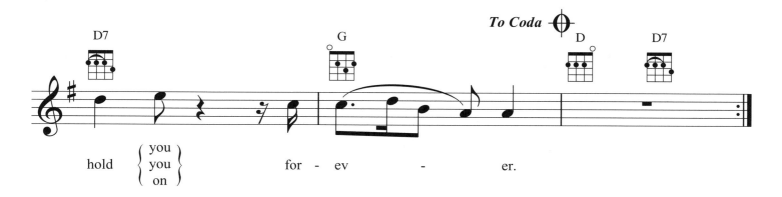

hold { you / you / on } for - ev - - er.

Interlude

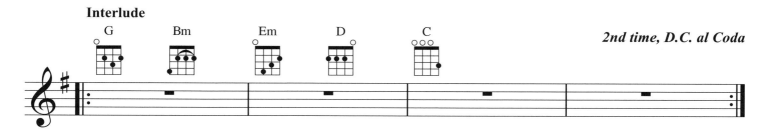

2nd time, D.C. al Coda

Coda

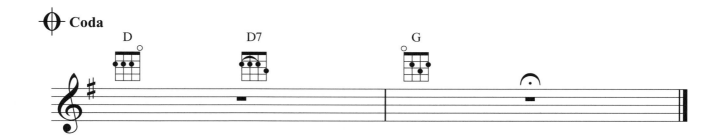

Additional Lyrics

2. When you kissed my lips with my mouth so full of questions,
   My worried mind, that you quiet.
   Place your hands on my face, close my eyes and say
   That love is a poor man's food, no prophesying.

3. So now we see how it is: this fist begets the spear;
   Weapons of war, symptoms of madness.
   Don't let your eyes refuse to see, don't let your ears refuse to hear.
   You ain't never gonna shake this sense of sadness.

How Can You Mend a Broken Heart

Words and Music by Barry Gibb and Robin Gibb

1. I can think of young-er days when liv-ing for my life was
2. I can still feel the breeze that rus-tles through the trees and

ev-'ry-thing a man could want to do.
mist-y mem-o-ries of days gone by.

I could nev-er see to-
We could nev-er see to-

mor-row,___ but I was nev-er told ___ a-bout ___ the sor-row.
mor-row;___ no one said a word ___ a-bout ___ the sor-row.

Chorus

And how can you mend ___ a bro-ken heart? ___

Copyright © 1971 by Universal Music Publishing International MGB Ltd., Warner-Tamerlane Publishing Corp. and Crompton Songs LLC
Copyright Renewed
All Rights for Universal Music Publishing International MGB Ltd. in the U.S. and Canada Administered by Universal Music - Careers
All Rights for Crompton Songs LLC Administered by Warner-Tamerlane Publishing Corp.
International Copyright Secured   All Rights Reserved

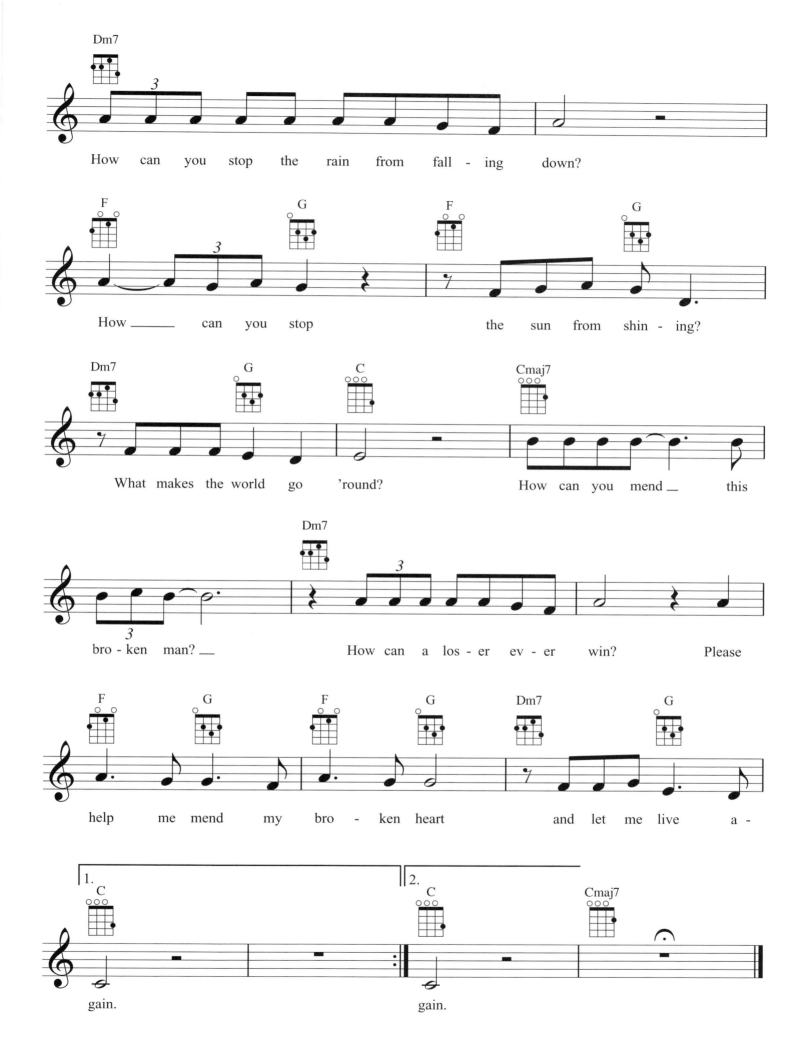

How can you stop the rain from fall - ing down?

How ____ can you stop the sun from shin - ing?

What makes the world go 'round? How can you mend __ this

bro - ken man? __ How can a los - er ev - er win? Please

help me mend my bro - ken heart and let me live a -

1. gain.

2. gain.

I Can See Clearly Now

Words and Music by Johnny Nash

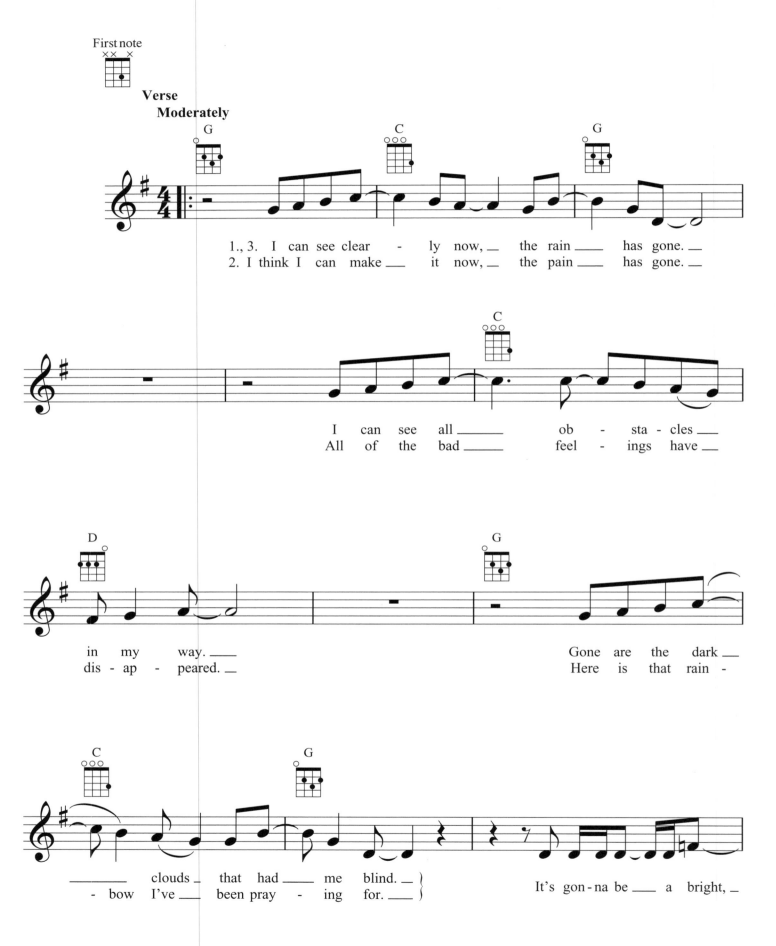

1., 3. I can see clear - ly now, ___ the rain ___ has gone. ___
2. I think I can make ___ it now, ___ the pain ___ has gone. ___

I can see all ___ ob - sta - cles ___
All of the bad ___ feel - ings have ___

in my way. ___
dis - ap - peared. ___

Gone are the dark
Here is that rain -

___ clouds ___ that had ___ me blind. ___
- bow I've ___ been pray - ing for. ___

It's gon - na be ___ a bright, ___

© 1972 (Renewed) NASHCO MUSIC
All Rights Reserved   Used by Permission

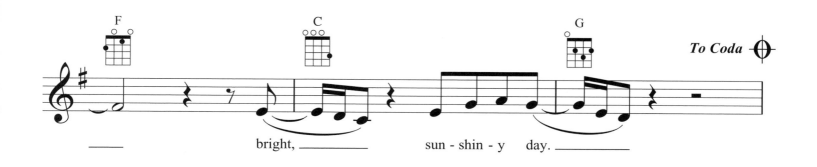

bright, _____ sun - shin - y day. _____

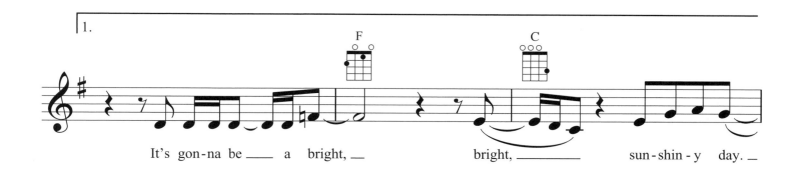

It's gon-na be ___ a bright, ___ bright, _____ sun-shin-y day. ___

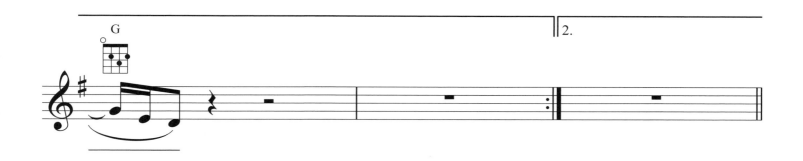

Look all a - round, _____ there's noth - ing but blue skies. _____

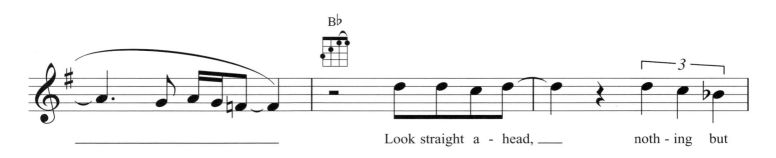

_____ Look straight a - head, ___ noth - ing but

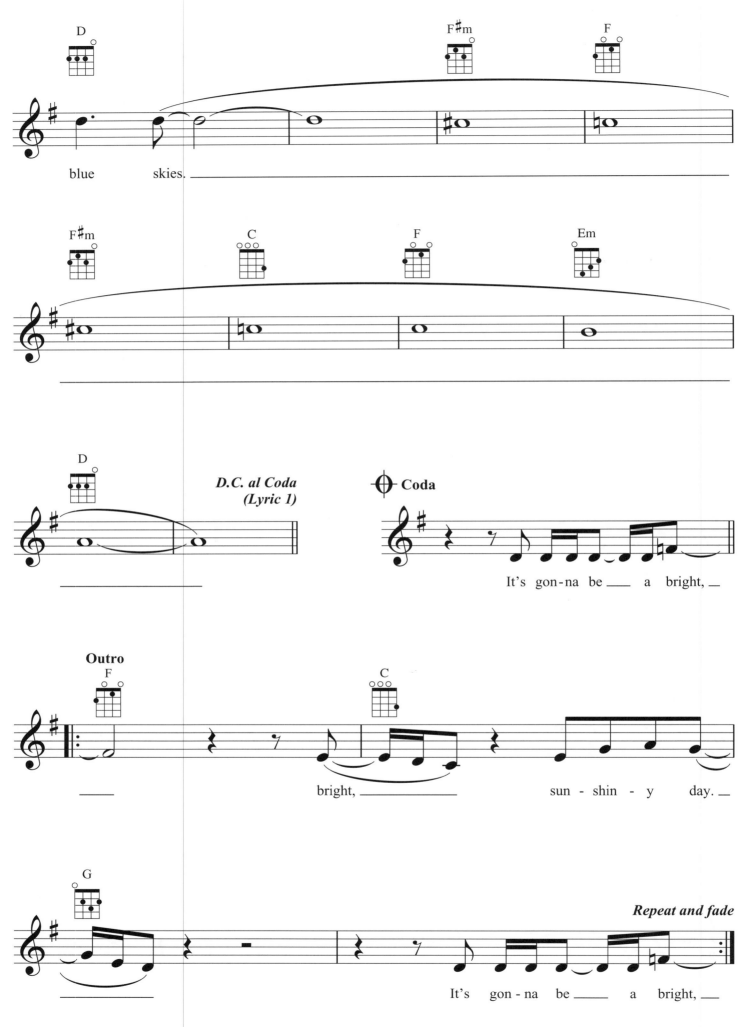

blue   skies. _____

_____

D.C. al Coda
(Lyric 1)

Coda

It's gon-na be ___ a   bright, ___

Outro

___   bright, _____   sun - shin - y   day. ___

Repeat and fade

It's   gon - na   be ___   a   bright, ___

I'll Be

Words and Music by Edwin McCain

© 1997 EMI APRIL MUSIC INC. and HARRINGTON PUBLISHING
All Rights Controlled and Administered by EMI APRIL MUSIC INC.
All Rights Reserved   International Copyright Secured   Used by Permission

Pre-Chorus

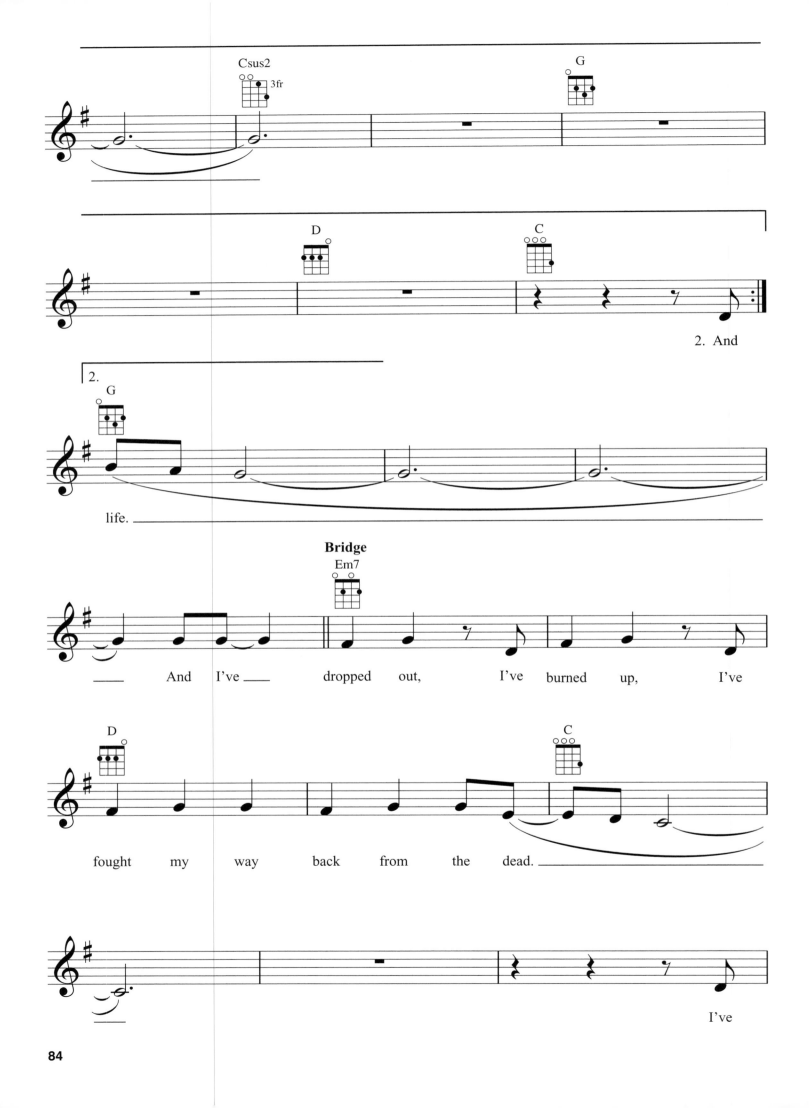

2. And

life.

Bridge

And I've ___ dropped out, I've burned up, I've

fought my way back from the dead.

I've

tuned in,   turned on,   re - mem - bered _____ the

thing   that   you   said. _____

D.S. al Coda

_____   **Outro Coda**

life, _____

the

great - est _____ fan of your _____ life.

I Will Wait

Words and Music by Mumford & Sons

Copyright © 2012 UNIVERSAL MUSIC PUBLISHING LTD.
All Rights in the U.S. and Canada Controlled and Administered by UNIVERSAL - POLYGRAM INTERNATIONAL TUNES, INC.
All Rights Reserved   Used by Permission

Chorus

*D
I will __ wait, I will __ wait for you.

* Let chord ring.

*A   *D
And I will __ wait, I will __ wait for you.

*F#m   *A   D
3. So break my __

Verse

D   G
__ step
(4.) __ seen   and re - lent.
      and him with less.

D
You for - gave, _____ and I won't
Now in some way _____ shake the ex -

A   1.   2.
for - get.
cess.   4. Know what we've __
                              'Cause

87

Island in the Sun

Words and Music by Rivers Cuomo

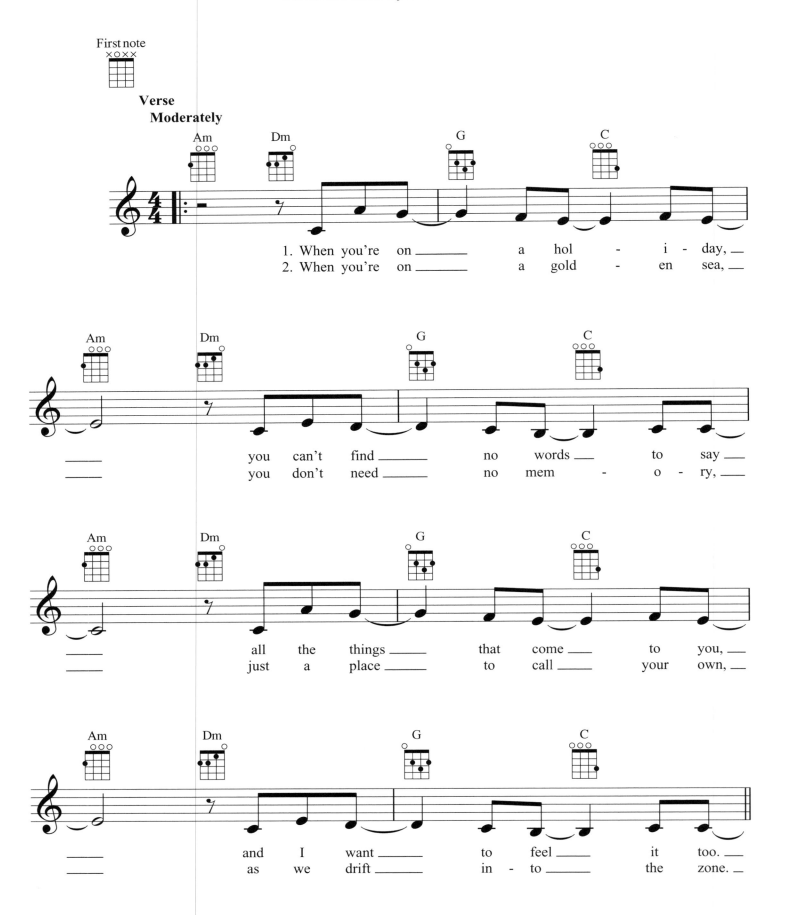

Copyright © 2001 E.O. Smith Music
International Copyright Secured All Rights Reserved

On an is - land in _____ the sun, _____

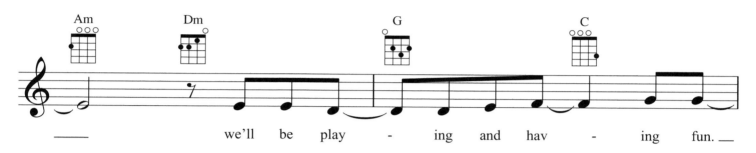

_____ we'll be play - ing and hav - ing fun. _____

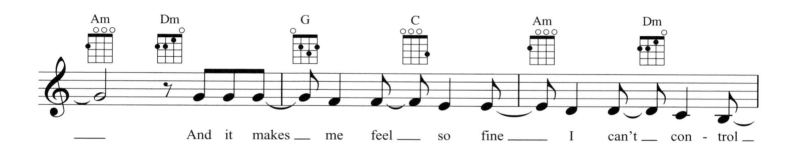

_____ And it makes _____ me feel _____ so fine _____ I can't _____ con - trol _____

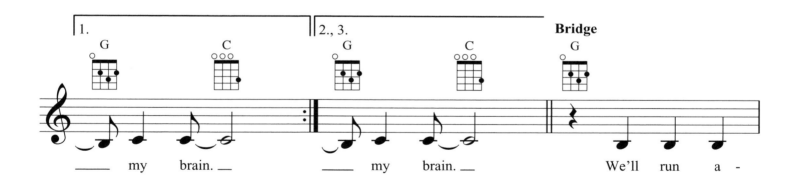

1.
_____ my brain. _____

2., 3.   **Bridge**
_____ my brain. _____   We'll run a -

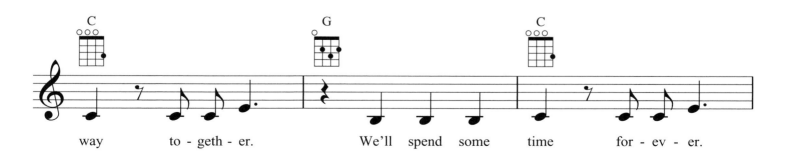

way   to - geth - er.   We'll spend some time   for - ev - er.

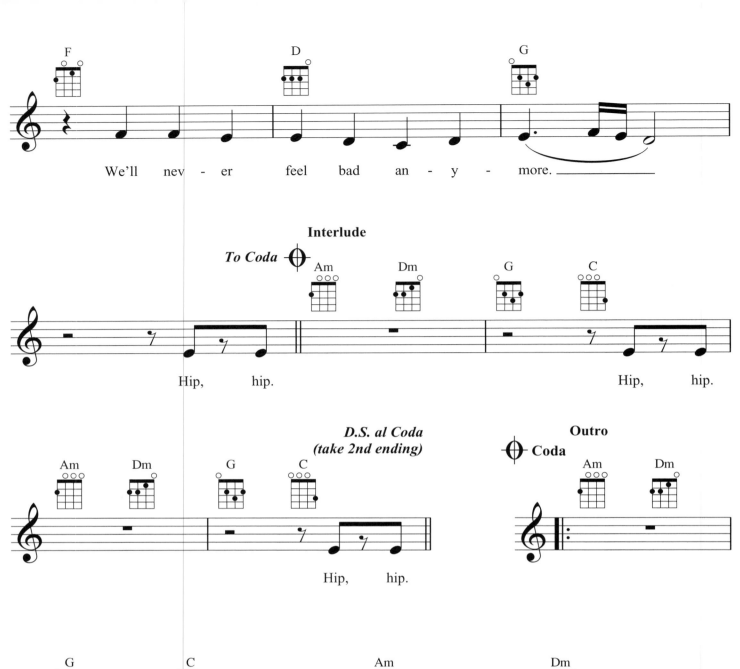

We'll nev - er feel bad an - y - more. _____

Interlude

To Coda ⊕

Hip, hip.   Hip, hip.

D.S. al Coda
(take 2nd ending)

⊕ **Coda**   **Outro**

Hip, hip.

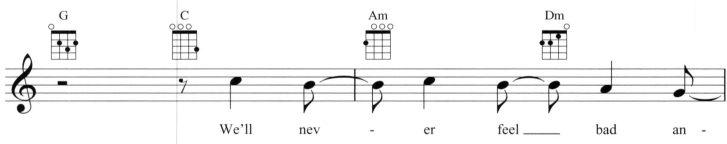

We'll nev - er feel _____ bad an -

Repeat and fade

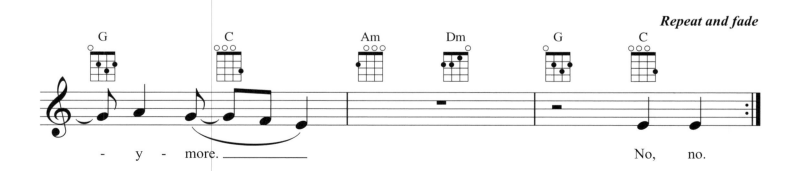

- y - more. _____   No, no.

Karma Police

Words and Music by Thomas Yorke, Jonathan Greenwood, Colin Greenwood, Edward O'Brien and Philip Selway

© 1997 WARNER CHAPPELL MUSIC LTD.
All Rights in the U.S. and Canada Administered by WB MUSIC CORP.
All Rights Reserved   Used by Permission

This is what ___ you'll get _____ when you mess _____ with us. ___

D.C. al Coda
(no repeat)

Coda

Outro

For a min - ute there, ___ I lost ___ my - self. ___

I lost _____ my - self. _____

Phew, for a min - ute there, _____ I lost _____ my - self. ___

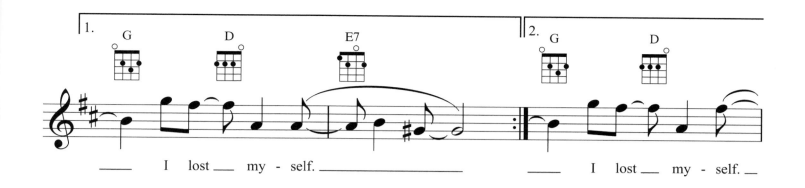

I lost my-self.   I lost my-self.

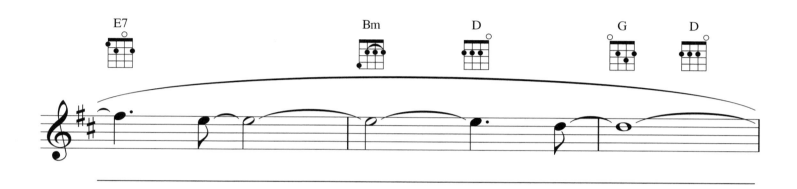

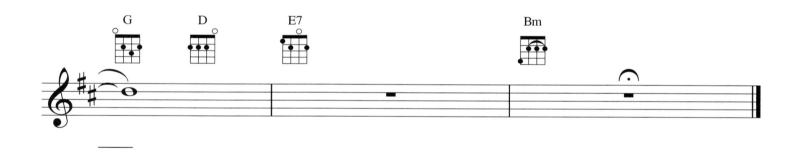

Additional Lyrics

2. Karma police, arrest this girl.
   Her Hitler hairdo is making me feel ill,
   And we have crashed her party.

3. Karma police, I've given all I can.
   It's not enough. I've given all I can,
   But we're still on the payroll.

Let Her Cry

**Words and Music by Darius Carlos Rucker, Everett Dean Felber,
Mark William Bryan and James George Sonefeld**

1. She sits a - lone by a lamp - post ____ tryin' to find a thought that's es - caped _ her mind. ____

She says, "Dad's _ the one I ____ love ____ the most, ____ but Stipe's _ not far be - hind." ____

2. She nev - er lets me in, ___ on - ly tells _ me where she's _ been ____

3., 4. *See additional lyrics*

© 1994 EMI APRIL MUSIC INC. and MONICA'S RELUCTANCE TO LOB
All Rights Controlled and Administered by EMI APRIL MUSIC INC.
All Rights Reserved   International Copyright Secured   Used by Permission

when she's had ___ too much to drink. _____

I say that I don't ___ care, ___ I just run my hands through her dark hair, ___ then I

pray to God, ___"You got-ta help me fly ___ a - way." ___ And just let her cry ___

Chorus

_____ if the tears ___ fall down ___ like rain. ___ Let her sing ___

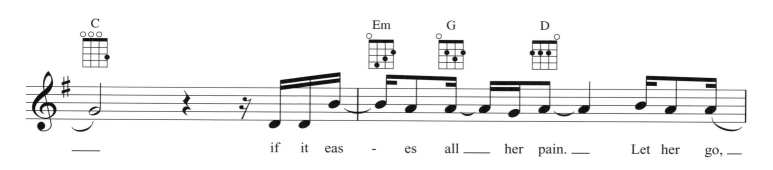

___ if it eas - es all ___ her pain. ___ Let her go, ___

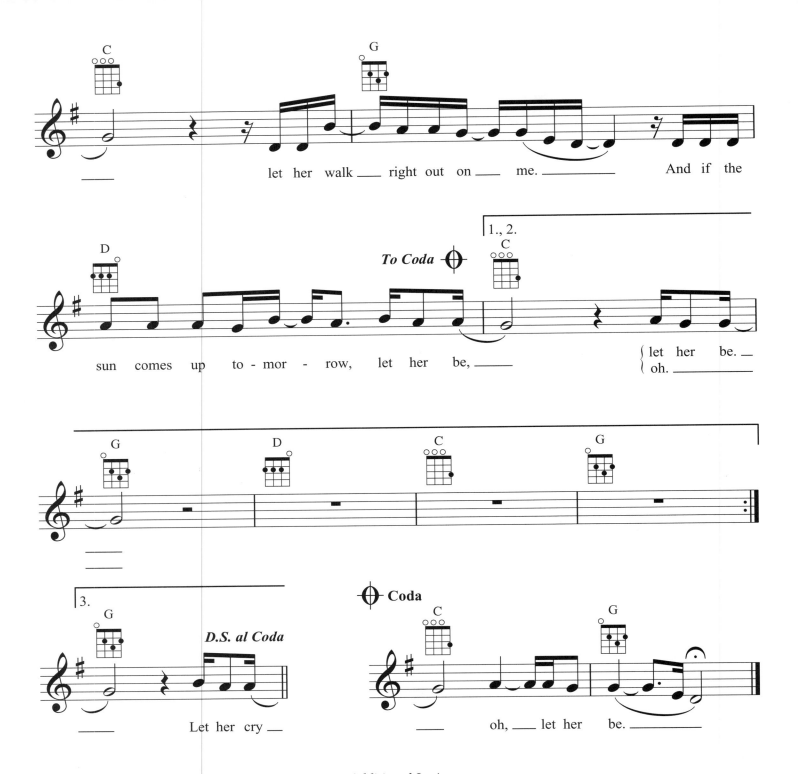

Additional Lyrics

3. This morning I woke up alone,
   Found a note standing by the phone
   Sayin', "Maybe, maybe I'll be back someday."
   I wanted to look for you; you walked in.
   I didn't know just what to do,
   So I sat back down, had a beer and felt sorry for myself.

4. Last night I tried to leave.
   Cried so much, I could not believe
   She was the same girl I fell in love with long ago.
   She went in the back to get high.
   I sat down on my couch and cried,
   Yelling, "Oh, Mama, please help me. Won't you hold my hand?"

Listen to the Music

Words and Music by Tom Johnston

First note

Verse
With a groove, in 2

1. Don't you feel __ it grow - ing day by __ day? __
2.–4. *See additional lyrics*

__ Peo - ple get - ting read - y for the

news. Some are hap - py, __ some are

sad. _____ Oh, _____ we got to let the mu - sic

1., 3.

play. __

© 1973 (Renewed) WARNER-TAMERLANE PUBLISHING CORP.
All Rights Reserved   Used by Permission

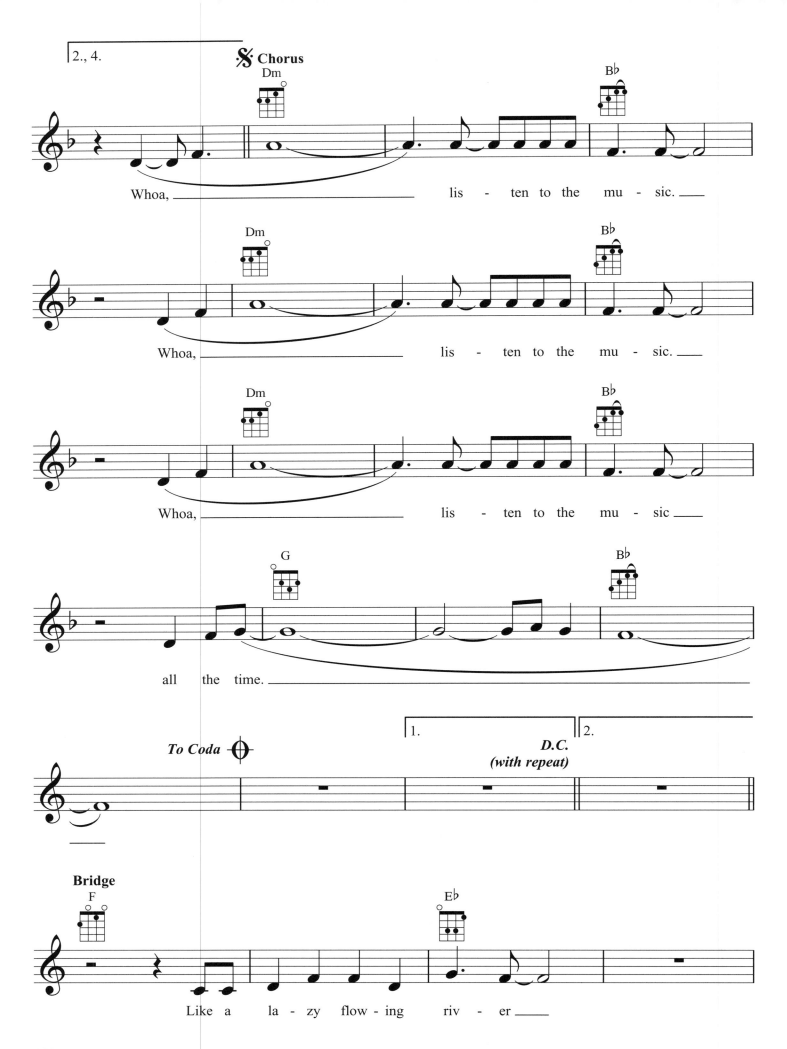

Whoa, _____ lis - ten to the mu - sic. _____

Whoa, _____ lis - ten to the mu - sic. _____

Whoa, _____ lis - ten to the mu - sic _____

all the time. _____

Like a la - zy flow - ing riv - er _____

100

sur - round - ing   cas - tles   in the sky. _____

And the   crowd   is   grow - ing   big - ger,

lis - t'ning   for   the   hap - py   sounds, __   and   I

D.S. al Coda

⊕ **Coda**

got   to   let ____ them   fly. _____   Whoa, _____

Additional Lyrics

2. What the people need is a way to make them smile.
   It ain't so hard to do if you know how.
   Got to get a message, get it on through.
   Oh, now mama's going to after 'while.

3. Well, I know you know better everything I say.
   Meet me in the country for a day.
   We'll be happy and we'll dance.
   Oh, we're gonna dance our blues away.

4. If I'm feeling good to you and you're feeling good to me,
   There ain't nothing we can't do or say.
   Feeling good, feeling fine.
   Oh, baby, let the music play.

Lodi

Words and Music by John Fogerty

First note

Verse

Moderately

1. Just a - bout a year a - go, _____ I

(2., 3.) *See additional lyrics*

set out on the road, _____ seek - ing my fame and for -

- tune and look - ing for a pot of gold. _____ Well,

things got bad, _____ and things got worse; _____ I guess you know the tune. _____

Copyright © 1969 Jondora Music
Copyright Renewed
International Copyright Secured All Rights Reserved

Chorus

_____ Oh, Lord, stuck in Lo - di a -

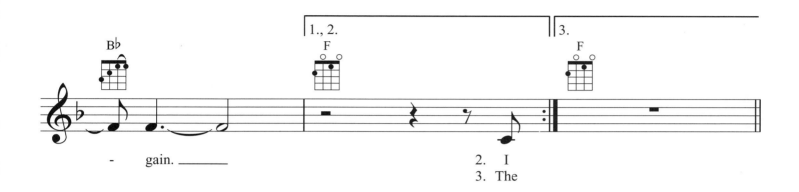

- gain. _____

1., 2.

2. I

3.

3. The

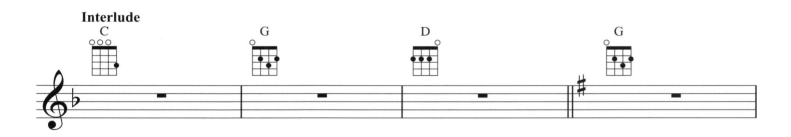

Interlude

Verse

4. If I on - ly had a dol - lar for

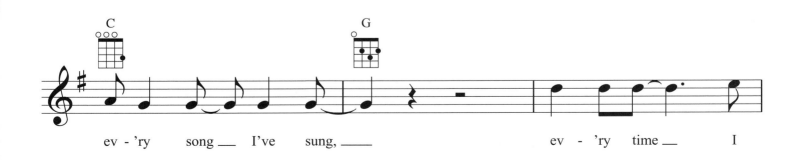

ev - 'ry song ___ I've sung, _____ ev - 'ry time ___ I

Additional Lyrics

2. I rode in on the Greyhound; well, I'll be walking out if I go.
   I was just passing through; must be seven months or more.
   I ran out of time and money; looks like they took my friends.

3. The man from the magazine said I was on my way.
   Somewhere, I lost connections; I ran out of songs to play.
   I came into town a one-night stand; looks like my plans fell through.

The Night They Drove Old Dixie Down

Words and Music by Robbie Robertson

© 1969 (Renewed) WB MUSIC CORP. and CANAAN MUSIC CORP.
All Rights Administered by WB MUSIC CORP.
All Rights Reserved   Used by Permission

night they drove old Dix - ie down _____ and all the

peo - ple were sing - ing. They went: Na na na

na na na, _____ na na na na na na _____ na na _____ na.

1., 2.   3.   Am

Additional Lyrics

2. Back with my wife in Tennessee, and one day she said to me,
   "Virgil, quick, come see. There goes Robert E. Lee."
   Now I don't mind, I'm chopping wood,
   And I don't care if the money's no good.
   Just take what you need and leave the rest,
   But they should never have taken the very best.

3. Like my father before me, I'm a working man.
   And like my brother before me, I took a rebel stand.
   But he was just eighteen, proud and brave,
   But a Yankee laid him in his grave.
   I swear by the blood below my feet,
   You can't raise a Caine back up when he's in defeat.

Losing My Religion

Words and Music by William Berry, Peter Buck, Michael Mills and Michael Stipe

© 1991 NIGHT GARDEN MUSIC
All Rights Administered by WARNER-TAMERLANE PUBLISHING CORP.
All Rights Reserved   Used by Permission

I set it _____ up. _____

Verse

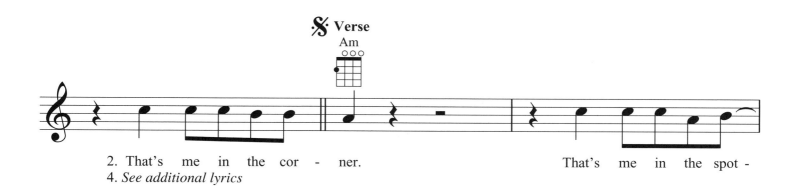

2. That's me in the cor - ner.
4. *See additional lyrics*

That's me in the spot -

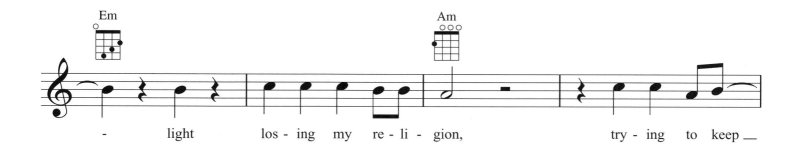

- light los - ing my re - li - gion,   try - ing to keep _____

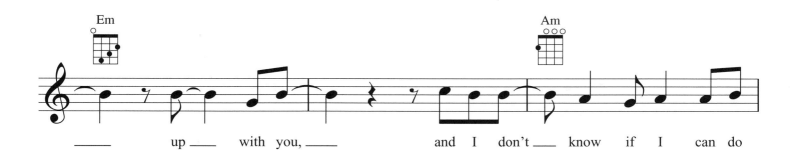

_____ up _____ with you, _____   and I don't _____ know if I can do

it.   Oh no, I've said too _____ much. _____   I

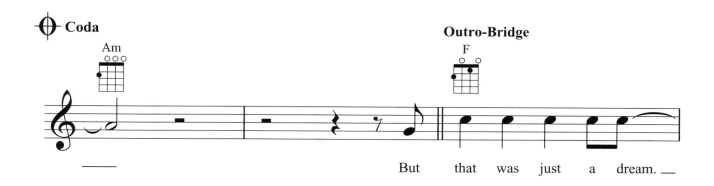

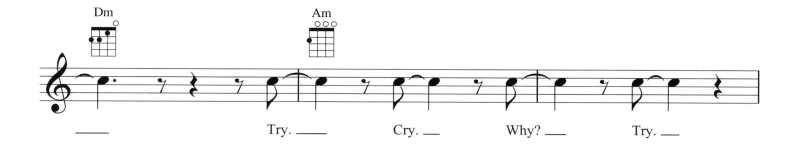

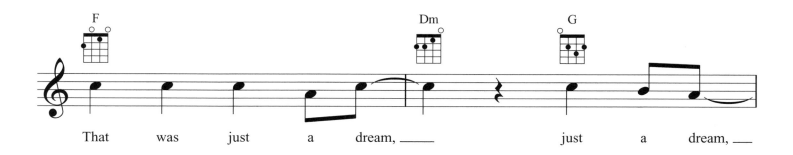

Additional Lyrics

3. Every whisper of ev'ry waking hour,
   I'm choosing my confessions,
   Trying to keep an eye on you like a hurt, lost and blinded fool.
   Oh no, I've said too much. I set it up.

4. Consider this, consider this the hint of the century.
   Consider this: the slip that brought me to my knees failed.
   What if all these fantasies come flailing around?
   And now I've said too much.

Lyin' Eyes

Words and Music by Don Henley and Glenn Frey

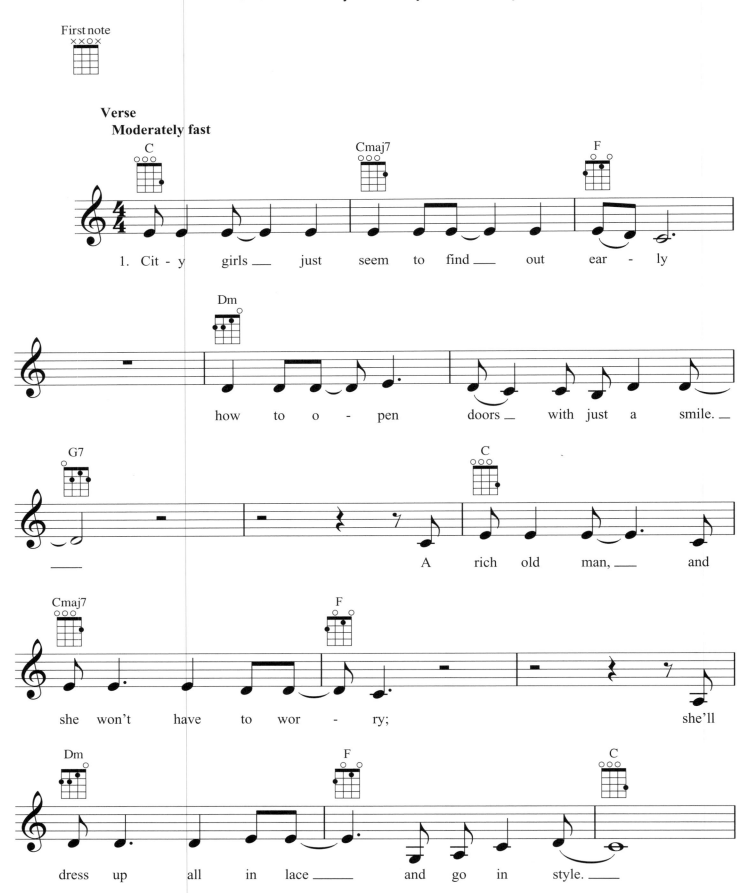

© 1975 (Renewed) CASS COUNTY MUSIC and RED CLOUD MUSIC
All Rights Administered by WARNER-TAMERLANE PUBLISHING CORP.
All Rights Reserved   Used by Permission

Verse

2. Late at night, ___ a big old house ___ gets lone-
3.–8. *See additional lyrics*

- ly. I guess ev-'ry form ___ of

ref - uge has its price. ___ And it

breaks her heart ___ to think her love ___ is on - ly

giv - en to a man ___ with hands ___ as cold as ice. ___

1., 3., 5., 6.

___

2., 4., 7.

3. So she ___
5., 7. She
8. My

Chorus

You can't hide _____ your ly - in' eyes, _____

* Let chord ring.

_____ and your smile _____

_____ is a thin ____ dis - guise. I thought by

now _____ you'd re - al - ize _____

_____ there ain't no way ____ to hide ____ your ly - in' eyes. ____

1.   D.S.
                                (with repeat)

2.   D.S. al Coda
                          (with repeats)

_____

4. On the

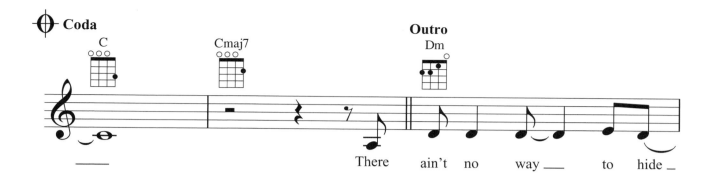

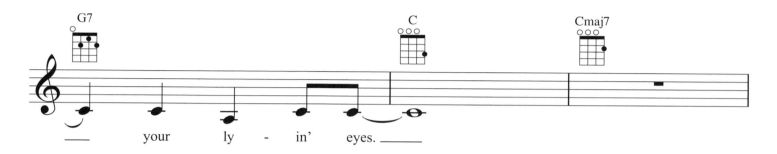

your ly - in' eyes. _____

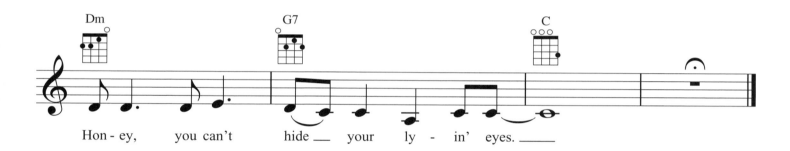

Hon - ey, you can't hide ___ your ly - in' eyes. _____

Additional Lyrics

3. So she tells him she must go out for the evening,
   To comfort an old friend who's feeling down.
   But he knows where she's going as she's leaving;
   She is headed for the cheating side of town.

4. On the other side of town, a boy is waiting
   With fiery eyes and dreams no one could steal.
   She drives on through the night anticipating,
   'Cause he makes her feel the way she used to feel.

5. She rushes to his arms; they fall together.
   She whispers that it's only for a while.
   She swears that soon she'll be coming back forever.
   She pulls away and leaves him with a smile.

6. She gets up and pours herself a strong one,
   And stares out at the stars up in the sky.
   Another night; it's gonna be a long one.
   She draws the shade and hangs her head to cry.

7. She wonders how it ever got this crazy;
   She thinks about a boy she knew in school.
   Did she get tired or did she just get lazy?
   She's so far gone, she feels just like a fool.

8. My, oh my, you sure know how to arrange things.
   You set it up so well, so carefully.
   Ain't it funny how your new life didn't change things?
   You're still the same old girl you used to be.

Maggie May

Words and Music by Rod Stewart and Martin Quittenton

Copyright © 1971 by Unichappell Music Inc., Rod Stewart and EMI Full Keel Music
Copyright Renewed 1999
All Rights for Rod Stewart Controlled and Administered by EMI Blackwood Music Inc.
International Copyright Secured   All Rights Reserved

home, just to save you from be-ing a-lone. You

stole my heart, — and that's what real-ly hurts.

|1.–3. |4. **Outro**

2. The (Instrumental)

Repeat and fade

Additional Lyrics

2. The morning sun, when it's in your face,
Really shows your age.
But that don't worry me none;
In my eyes, you're everything.
I laughed at all of your jokes.
My love you didn't need to coax.
Oh, Maggie, I couldn't have tried any more.

Chorus: You led me away from home
Just to save you from being alone.
You stole my soul,
And that's a pain I can do without.

3. All I needed was a friend
To lend a guiding hand.
But you turned into a lover and, mother, what a lover!
You wore me out.
All you did was wreck my bed,
And in the morning, kick me in the head.
Oh, Maggie, I couldn't have tried any more.

Chorus: You led me away from home
'Cause you didn't want to be alone.
You stole my heart;
I couldn't leave you if I tried.

4. I suppose I could collect my books
And get on back to school,
Or steal my daddy's cue
And make a living out of playing pool.
Or find myself a rock 'n' roll band
That needs a helping hand.
Oh, Maggie, I wish I'd never seen your face.

Chorus: You made a first-class fool out of me,
But I'm as blind as a fool can be.
You stole my heart, but I love you anyway.

Me and You and a Dog Named Boo

Words and Music by Lobo

Copyright © 1971 Sony/ATV Music Publishing LLC
Copyright Renewed
All Rights Administered by Sony/ATV Music Publishing LLC, 424 Church Street, Suite 1200, Nashville, TN 37219
International Copyright Secured   All Rights Reserved

back on the road — a - gain. —

Chorus

Me and you ____ and a dog ____ named Boo, ____

trav -'lin' and a - liv - in' off the land. Me and you ____ and a dog __

To Coda

1., 2.

____ named Boo; — how I love — be - in' a free man.

3.

D.S. al Coda

Coda

2. Now, man.
3. Now, I'll

Additional Lyrics

2. Now, I can still recall the wheat fields of St. Paul
   And the mornin' we got caught robbin' from an old hen.
   Old MacDonald, he made us work, but then he paid us for what it was worth.
   Another tank of gas and back on the road again.

3. Now, I'll never forget the day we motored stately into big L. A.
   The lights of the city put settlin' down in my brain.
   Though it's only been a month or so, that old car's buggin' us to go.
   We gotta get away and get back on the road again.

No Rain

Words and Music by Blind Melon

© 1992 EMI APRIL MUSIC INC. and HEAVY MELON MUSIC
All Rights Controlled and Administered by EMI APRIL MUSIC INC.
All Rights Reserved   International Copyright Secured   Used by Permission

It's ___ not sane. _____

Chorus

I just want some - one to say to me, ___ oh, ___

_____ I'll al-ways be ___ there when ___ you wake, ___

yeah. ___ You know I'd like to keep ___

___ my cheeks ___ dry to - day. ___

To Coda

So stay with me ___ and I'll have it made. ___

es - cape, _____ es - cape. _____

Verse

_____ 3. All I can say ___ is that my life is pret - ty plain. ___

___ You don't like my point of view; ___ you think that I'm in -

sane. It's ___ not sane, _____

D.S. al Coda

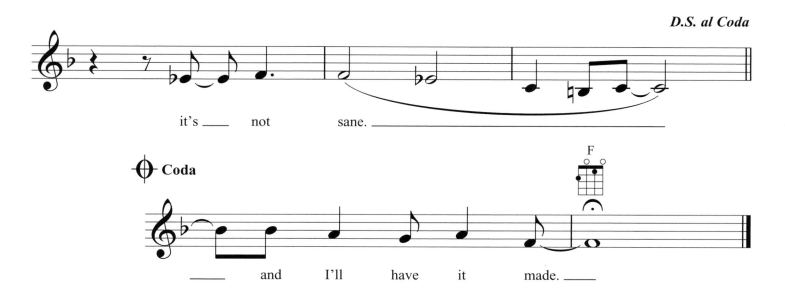

it's ___ not sane. _____

Coda

_____ and I'll have it made. ___

Norwegian Wood
(This Bird Has Flown)

Words and Music by John Lennon and Paul McCartney

Copyright © 1965 Sony/ATV Music Publishing LLC
Copyright Renewed
All Rights Administered by Sony/ATV Music Publishing LLC, 424 Church Street, Suite 1200, Nashville, TN 37219
International Copyright Secured   All Rights Reserved

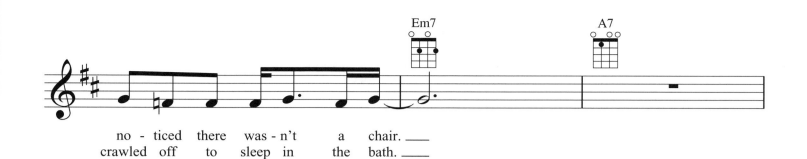

no - ticed there was - n't a chair. ____
crawled off to sleep in the bath. ____

Verse

2. I sat on a rug, bid - ing my time, drink - ing her wine.
4. And when I a - woke, I was a - lone; this bird had flown.

1.

We talked un - til two, and then she said, "It's time for bed." _
So, I lit a fire, is - n't it

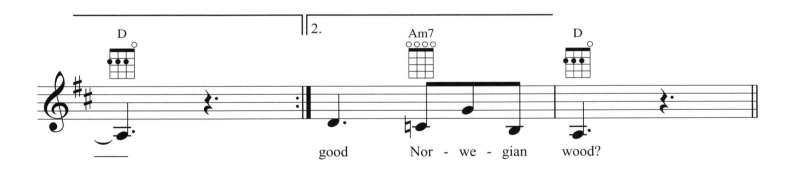

2.

good Nor - we - gian wood?

Outro

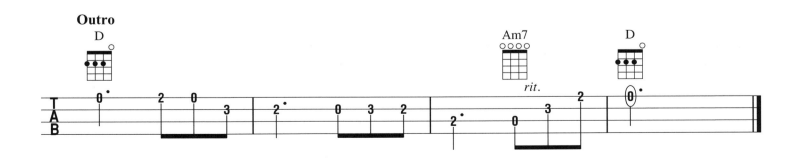

Photograph

Lyrics by Chad Kroeger
Music by Nickelback

© 2005 WARNER-TAMERLANE PUBLISHING CORP., ARM YOUR DILLO PUBLISHING INC., ZERO-G MUSIC, INC.,
BLACK DIESEL MUSIC, INC. and DANIEL ADAIR PUBLISHING DESIGNEE
All Rights Administered by WARNER-TAMERLANE PUBLISHING CORP.
All Rights Reserved   Used by Permission

And this is where I went ___ to school.
We used to lis - ten to the ra - di - o

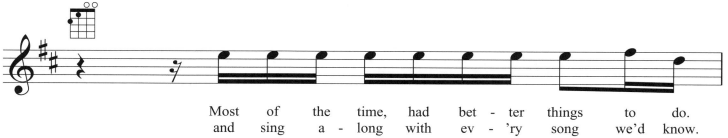

Most of the time, had bet - ter things to do.
and sing a - long with ev - 'ry song we'd know.

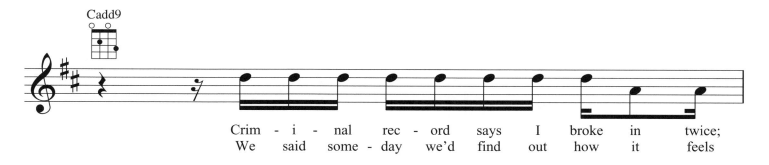

Crim - i - nal rec - ord says I broke in twice;
We said some - day we'd find out how it feels

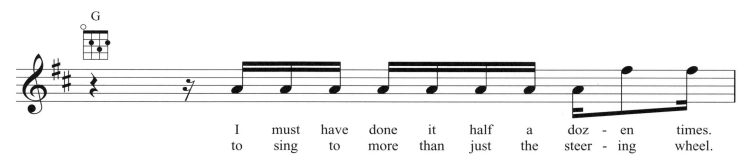

I must have done it half a doz - en times.
to sing to more than just the steer - ing wheel.

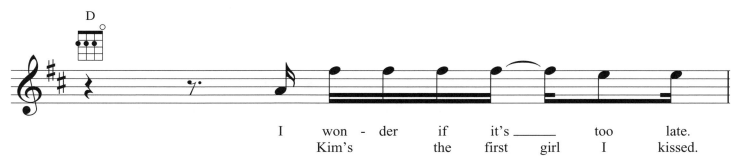

I won - der if it's ___ too late.
Kim's the first girl I kissed.

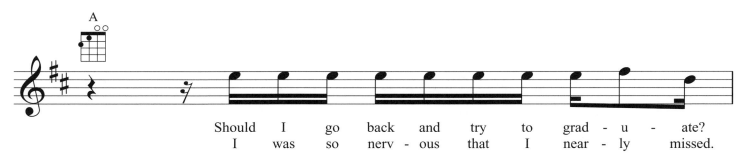

Should I go back and try to grad - u - ate?
I was so nerv - ous that I near - ly missed.

mem - o - ry of walk - ing out the front door, I found the

pho - to of the friend that I was look - ing for. It's

To Coda

1.

hard to say it, time to say it: Good - bye, ____ good - bye. ____

2.

Good - bye, ____ good - bye. _____

Bridge

I miss that town, ____ I miss their fac - es. You can't e - rase, ____

____ you can't re - place ____ it. I miss it now, ____ I can't be - lieve ____

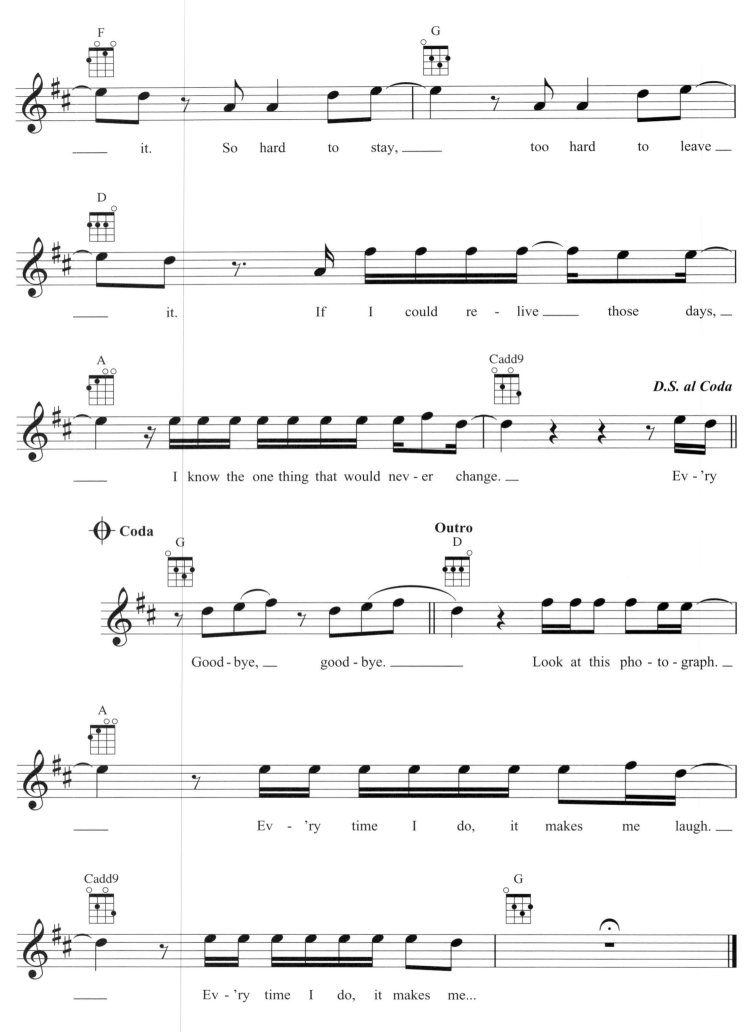

F   G

_____ it.   So   hard   to   stay, _____   too   hard   to   leave _____

D

_____ it.   If   I   could   re - live _____ those   days, __

A   Cadd9

D.S. al Coda

_____ I know the one thing that would nev - er   change. __   Ev - 'ry

Coda

G   **Outro**
                                D

Good - bye, __   good - bye. _____   Look at this pho - to - graph. __

A

_____   Ev - 'ry   time   I   do,   it   makes   me   laugh. __

Cadd9   G

_____   Ev - 'ry   time   I   do,   it   makes   me...

Patience

Words and Music by W. Axl Rose, Slash, Izzy Stradlin', Duff McKagan and Steven Adler

Copyright © 1988 Guns N' Roses Music (ASCAP) and Black Frog Music (ASCAP)
All Rights for Black Frog Music in the U.S. and Canada Controlled and Administered by Universal - PolyGram International Publishing, Inc.
International Copyright Secured   All Rights Reserved

There is no doubt _____ you're in _____ my heart _____ now. *(Instrumental)*

Chorus

Said, "Wom - an, take it slow. ____ It - 'll work it - self _____ out fine. _____ All we need ____ is just a lit - tle pa - tience." *(Instrumental)* Said, "Sug - ar,

make it slow ___ and we come to-geth - er fine. ___

All we need ___ is just _____ a lit - tle pa -

- tience." *(Instrumental)*

Additional Lyrics

2. I sit here on the stairs 'cause I'd rather be alone.
   If I can't have you right now, I'll wait, dear.
   Sometimes I get so tense, but I can't speed up the time.
   But you know, love, there's one more thing to consider.

Chorus: Said, "Woman, take it slow, and things will be just fine.
   You and I'll just use a little patience."
   Said, "Sugar, take the time 'cause the lights are shining bright.
   You and I've got what it takes to make it.
   We won't fake it.
   Ah, I'll never break it.
   'Cause I can't take it."

Rainy Day People

Words and Music by Gordon Lightfoot

1. Rain - y day peo - ple al - ways seem to know when it's
2. If you get lone - ly, all you real - ly need is that
3. *Instrumental*
4. Rain - y day peo - ple al - ways seem to know when you're

time to call. ___   Rain - y day peo - ple don't
rain - y day love. ___   Rain - y day peo - ple all
feel - in' blue. ___   High - step - pin' strut - ters who

talk; they just lis - ten till they've heard it all. ___
know there's no sor - row they can't rise a - bove. ___
End instrumental
land in the gut - ter some - times need one, too. ___

Rain - y day lov - ers don't lie when they tell ya   they been down ___ like
Rain - y day lov - ers don't love an - y oth - ers;   that would not ___ be
Rain - y day lov - ers don't lie when they tell ya   they been down ___ there,
Take it or leave it or try to be - lieve it   if you been down too

© 1974 (Renewed) MOOSE MUSIC LTD.
All Rights Reserved   Used by Permission

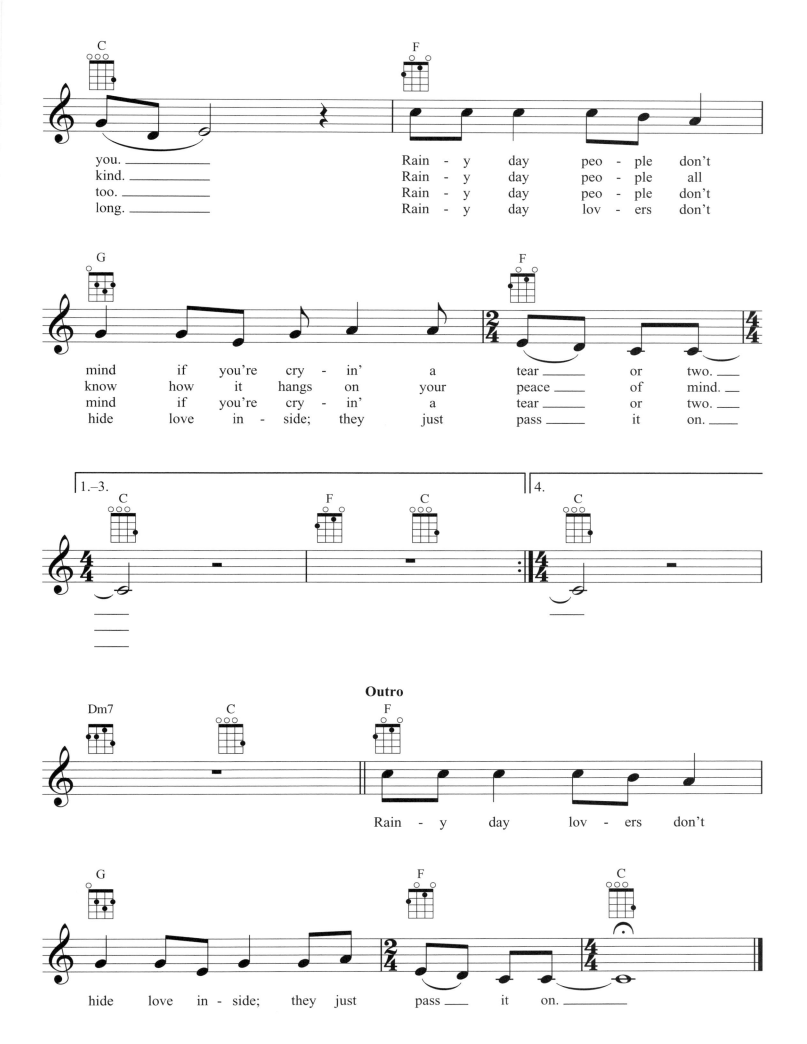

you. _____
kind. _____
too. _____
long. _____

Rain - y day peo - ple don't
Rain - y day peo - ple all
Rain - y day peo - ple don't
Rain - y day lov - ers don't

mind if you're cry - in' a tear _____ or two. ___
know how it hangs on your peace _____ of mind. ___
mind if you're cry - in' a tear _____ or two. ___
hide love in - side; they just pass _____ it on. ___

1.–3.   4.

Outro

Rain - y day lov - ers don't

hide love in - side; they just pass _____ it on. ___

Rhythm of Love

Words and Music by Tim Lopez

© 2010 WB MUSIC CORP. and SONGS FOR WHITNEY PUBLISHING
All Rights Administered by WB MUSIC CORP.
All Rights Reserved Used by Permission

Additional Lyrics

2. Well, my heart beats like a drum,
   A guitar string to the strum,
   A beautiful song to be sung.
   She's got blue eyes, deep like the sea,
   That roll back when she's laughing at me.
   She rises up like the tide the moment her lips meet mine.

D.S. And long after I've gone, you'll still be humming along.
   And I will keep you in my mind, the way you make love so fine.

She Talks to Angels

Words and Music by Chris Robinson and Rich Robinson

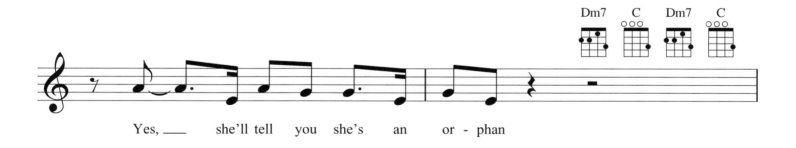

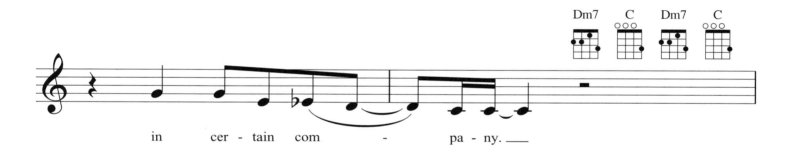

© 1991 WARNER-TAMERLANE PUBLISHING CORP.
All Rights Reserved   Used by Permission

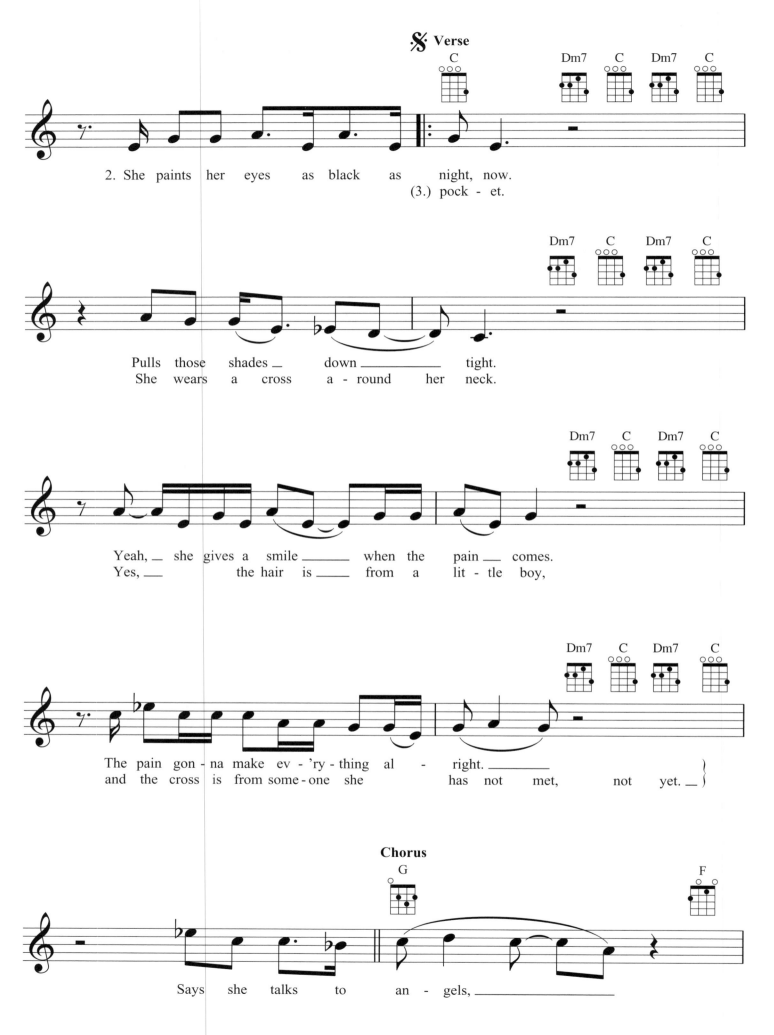

they call her out by _____ her name. _____

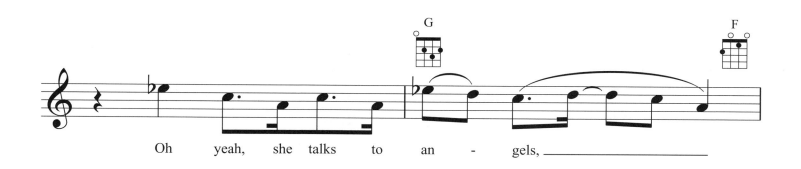

Oh yeah, she talks to an - gels, _____

To Coda ⊕

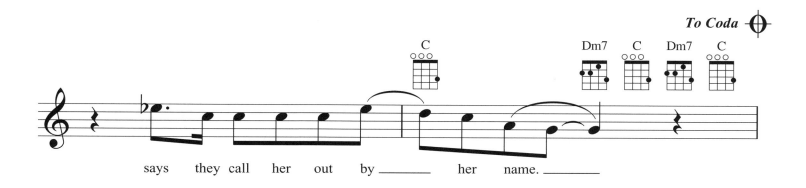

says they call her out by _____ her name. _____

1.

2.

3. She keeps a lock of hair in her

Bridge

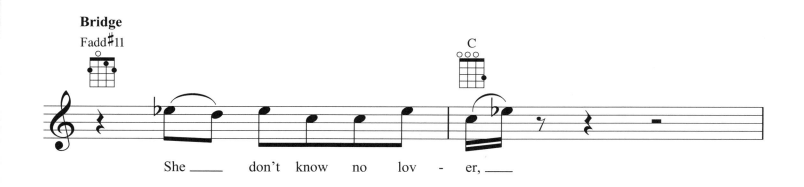

She _____ don't know no lov - er, _____

141

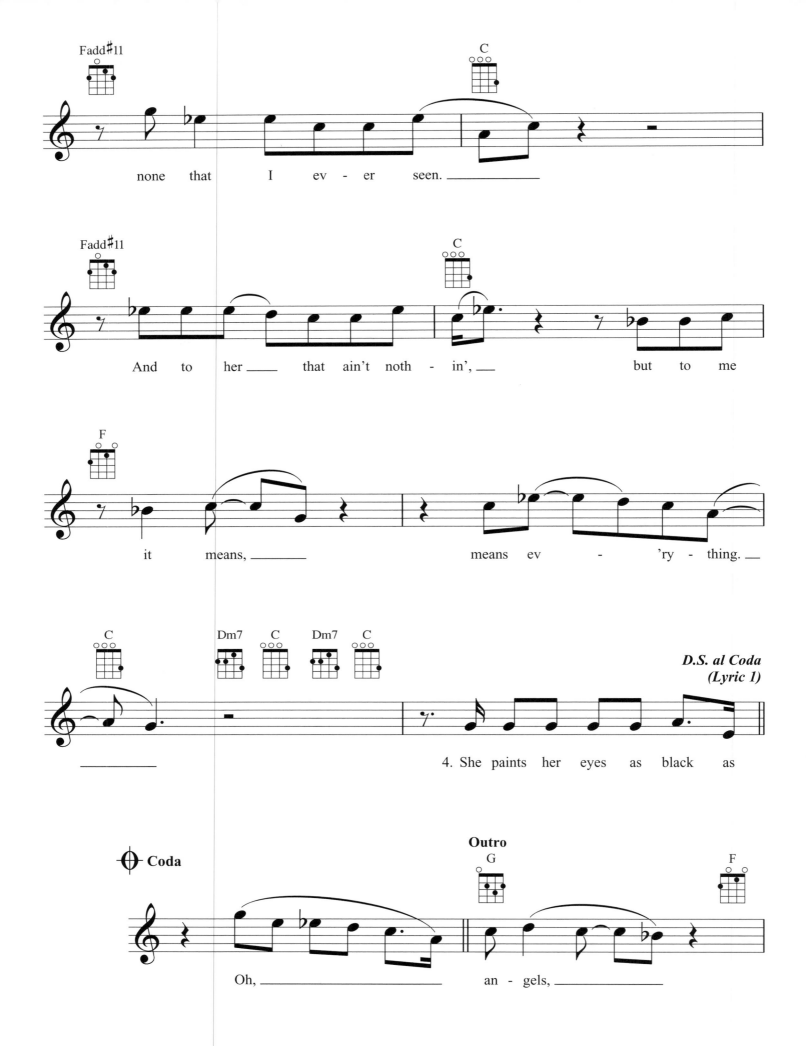

none that I ev - er seen. ____

And to her ____ that ain't noth - in', ____ but to me

it means, _____ means ev - 'ry - thing. __

____

D.S. al Coda
(Lyric 1)

4. She paints her eyes as black as

Outro

Oh, _____ an - gels, ____

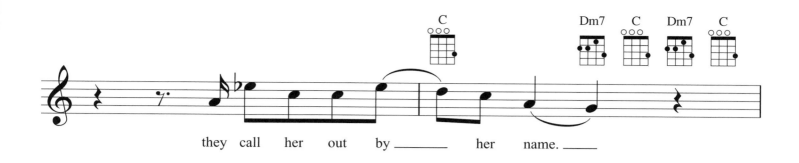

they call her out by _____ her name. _____

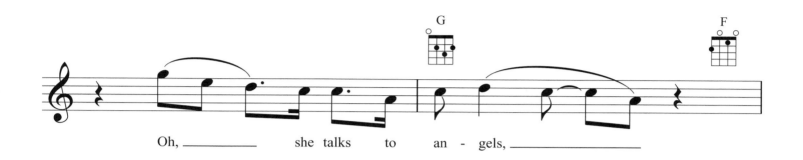

Oh, _____ she talks to an - gels, _____

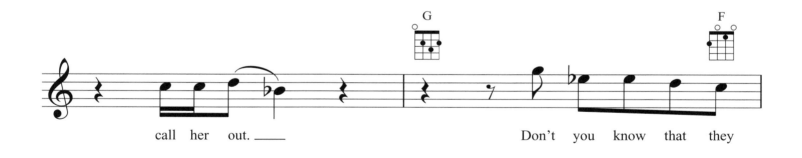

they call her out, _____ yeah, yeah, _____

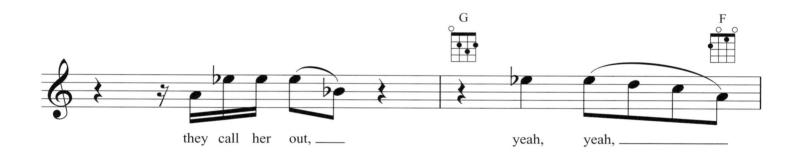

call her out. _____ Don't you know that they

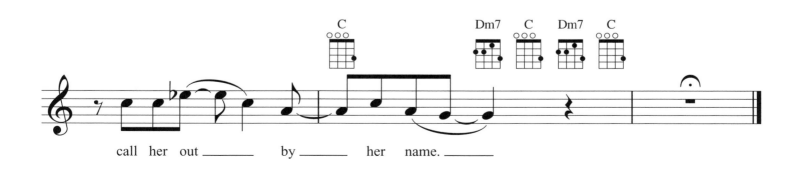

call her out _____ by _____ her name. _____

Shelter from the Storm

Words and Music by Bob Dylan

First note

Verse
Moderately, in 2

1. 'Twas in an-oth-er life-time, one of toil and
2.–10. *See additional lyrics*

blood, when black-ness was a vir-tue and the road was full of mud. __

__ I came in from the wil-der-ness, __ a

crea-ture void __ of form. __ "Come in," she said, "I'll give ya

shel-ter from __ the storm."

Copyright © 1974, 1976 Ram's Horn Music
International Copyright Secured   All Rights Reserved

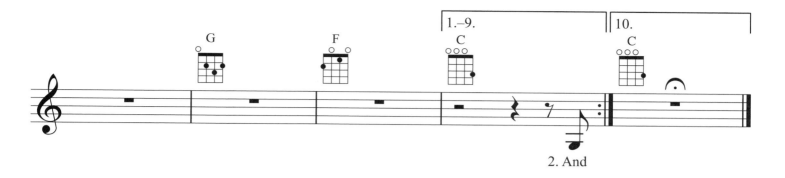

2. And

Additional Lyrics

2. And if I pass this way again, you can rest assured
   I'll always do my best for her; on that I give my word.
   In a world of steel-eyed death and men who are fighting to be warm,
   "Come in," she said, "I'll give ya shelter from the storm."

3. Not a word was spoke between us; there was little risk involved.
   Everything up to that point had been left unresolved.
   Try imagining a place where it's always safe and warm.
   "Come in," she said, "I'll give ya shelter from the storm."

4. I was burned out from exhaustion, buried in the hail,
   Poisoned in the bushes and blown out on the trail,
   Hunted like a crocodile, ravaged in the corn.
   "Come in," she said, "I'll give ya shelter from the storm."

5. Suddenly, I turned around and she was standin' there
   With silver bracelets on her wrists and flowers in her hair.
   She walked up to me so gracefully and took my crown of thorns.
   "Come in," she said, "I'll give ya shelter from the storm."

6. Now there's a wall between us; somethin' there's been lost.
   I took too much for granted; I got my signals crossed.
   Just to think that it all began on a non-eventful morn.
   "Come in," she said, "I'll give ya shelter from the storm."

7. Well, the deputy walks on hard nails and the preacher rides a mount,
   But nothing really matters much; it's doom alone that counts.
   And the one-eyed undertaker, he blows a futile horn.
   "Come in," she said, "I'll give ya shelter from the storm."

8. I've heard newborn babies wailin' like a mournin' dove
   And old men with broken teeth stranded without love.
   Do I understand your question, man? Is it hopeless and forlorn?
   "Come in," she said, "I'll give ya shelter from the storm."

9. In a little hilltop village, they gambled for my clothes.
   I bargained for salvation and she gave me a lethal dose.
   I offered up my innocence; I got repaid with scorn.
   "Come in," she said, "I'll give ya shelter from the storm."

10. Well, I'm livin' in a foreign country, but I'm bound to cross the line.
    Beauty walks a razor's edge; someday I'll make it mine.
    If I could only turn back the clock to when God and her were born.
    "Come in," she said, "I'll give ya shelter from the storm."

Small Town

Words and Music by John Mellencamp

© 1985 EMI FULL KEEL MUSIC
All Rights Reserved   International Copyright Secured   Used by Permission

my par - ents live in the same _____ small town. _____
had my-self a ball in a small _____ small town. _____

My job _____ is so small _____ town, pro - vides
Mar -ried an L. A. doll and brought her to this small town, now

lit - tle op - por - tu - ni - ties. _____
she's small town _ just like _____ me. _

Bridge

No, I can-not for - get _____ where it is _____ that I _____ come from, I

can-not for-get the peo-ple who love _____ me. Yeah, I can be my - self _____ here in

this small town, _ and peo-ple let _____ me be _____ just what I want to be.

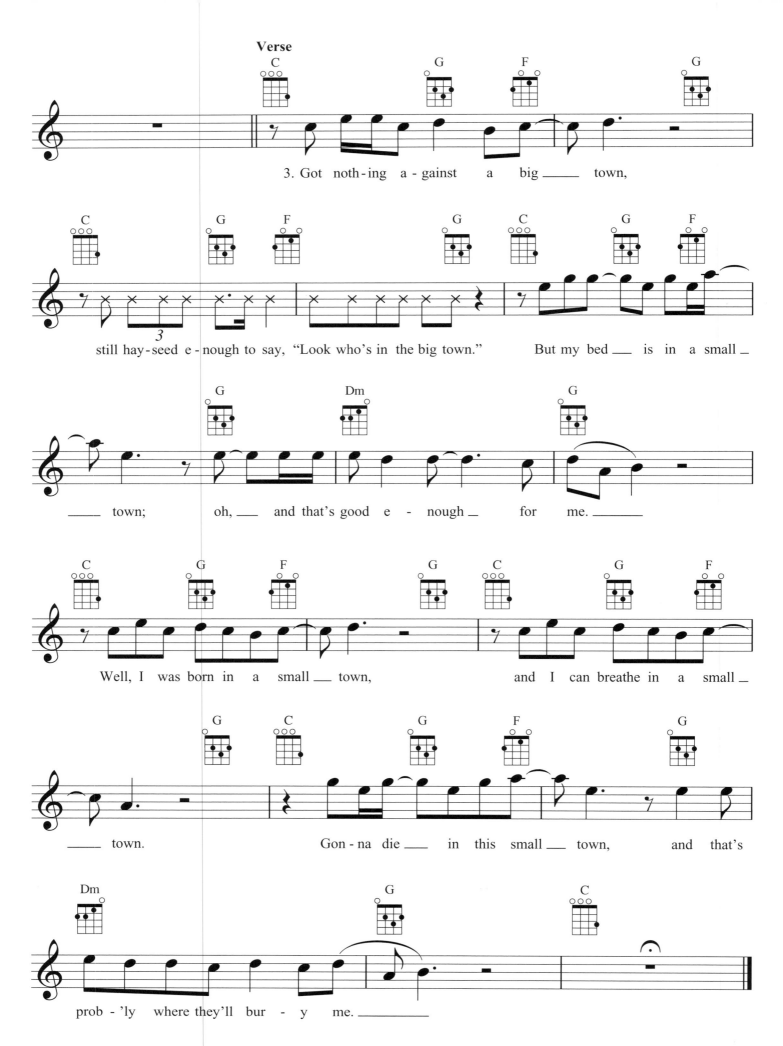

Shower the People

Words and Music by James Taylor

© 1975 (Renewed) COUNTRY ROAD MUSIC, INC.
All Rights Reserved   Used by Permission

oth - er; _____ it does - n't take an - y sac - ri - fice. _
way that you feel, you can feel it be - gin - ning to ease. _

___ Oh, _____ fa - ther and moth - er, sis -
___ I think it's true what they say a - bout the

ter and broth - er, if it feels nice ____ don't _
squeak - y wheel, _____ al - ways get - ting the grease. _

Chorus

___ think twice. _ Just show - er the peo - ple you love _
___ Bet - ter ____ to show - er the peo - ple you love _

___ with love; ___ show them the way ___ that you feel. _
___ with love; ___ show them the way ___ that you feel. _

_____ Things are gon - na work out fine ____ if you on - ly will. ____
_____ Things are gon - na be just fine ____ if you on - ly will. _

Show - er the peo - ple you love ___

___ with love; ___ show them the way ___ you feel. ___

___ Things are gon - na be much bet - ter if you on - ly will. ___

1. 2.

Outro-Chorus

Show - er the peo - ple you love ___ with love. ___

Repeat and fade

Show them the way ___ that you feel. ___

To Be with You

Words and Music by Eric Martin and David Grahame

© 1991 EMI APRIL MUSIC INC., DOG TURNER MUSIC and ERIC MARTIN SONGS
All Rights Controlled and Administered by EMI APRIL MUSIC INC.
All Rights Reserved   International Copyright Secured   Used by Permission

Chorus

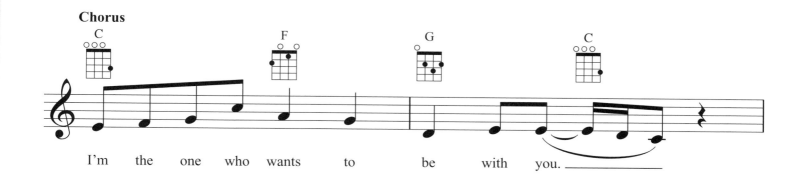

I'm the one who wants to be with you. _____

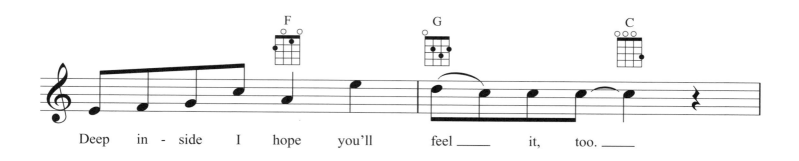

Deep in - side I hope you'll feel _____ it, too. _____

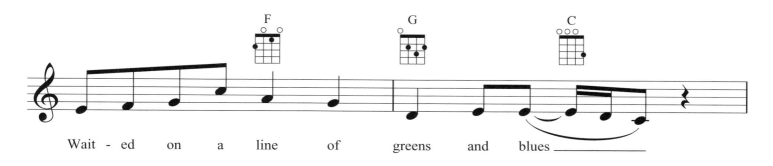

Wait - ed on a line of greens and blues _____

To Coda ⊕ |1.

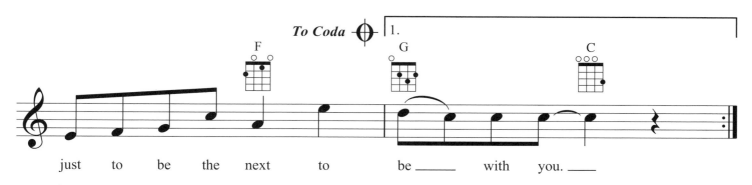

just to be the next to be _____ with you. _____

|2.   **Bridge**

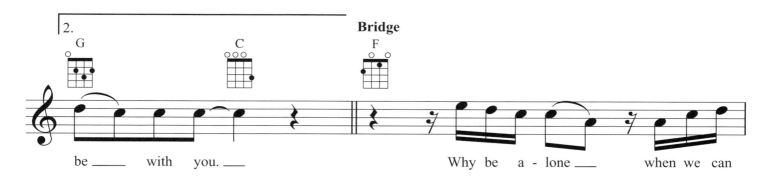

be _____ with you. _____   Why be a - lone _____ when we can

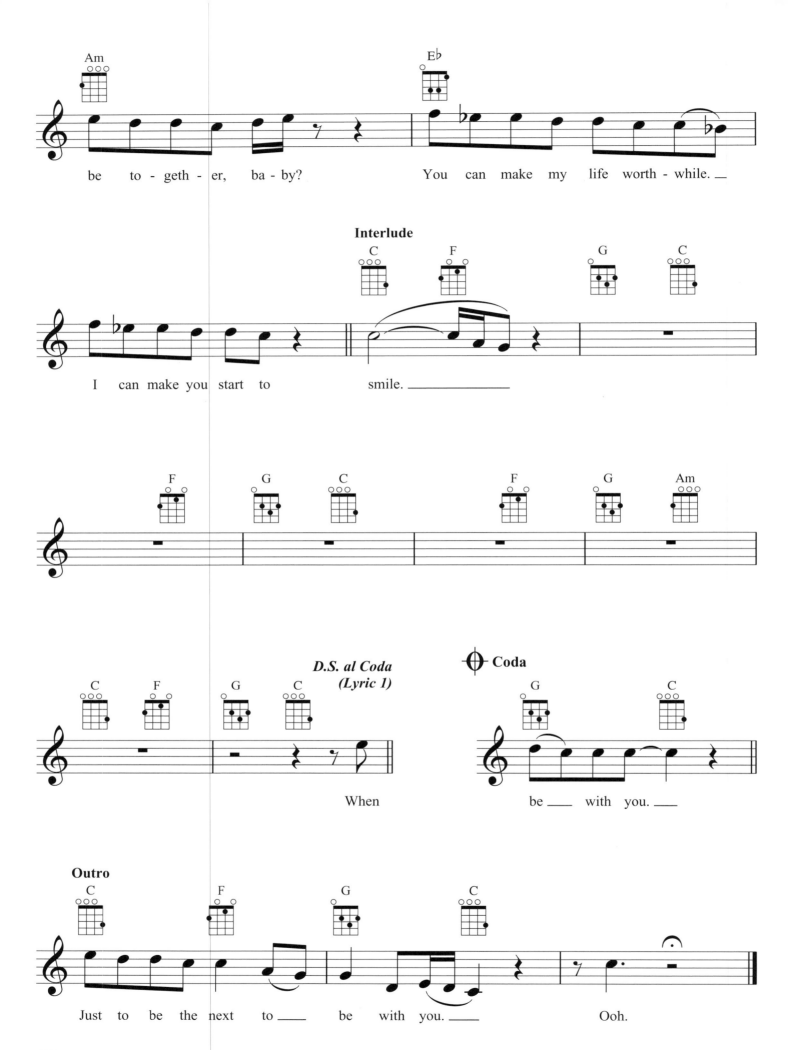

be to - geth - er, ba - by? You can make my life worth - while. ___

Interlude

I can make you start to smile. _____

D.S. al Coda
(Lyric 1)

When

Coda

be ___ with you. ___

Outro

Just to be the next to ___ be with you. ___ Ooh.

Tuesday's Gone

Words and Music by Allen Collins and Ronnie Van Zant

Copyright © 1973 SONGS OF UNIVERSAL, INC.
Copyright Renewed
All Rights Reserved   Used by Permission

Oh, my ba-by's gone _____ with the wind. _____

Verse

2. And I don't know,
3. Train _____ roll on

oh, _____ where I'm go - in'.
man - y miles from my home.

I just want to be _____ left a-
See, I'm rid - ing my _____ blues a-

lone. _____
way. _____

Well, when this train ends,
Tues - day, you see,

I'll _____ try a - gain. _____
she had to be free. _____

I'm leav - ing my wom - an _____ at
But some - how, I've got to _____ car-

Uncle John's Band

Words by Robert Hunter
Music by Jerry Garcia

© 1970 (Renewed) ICE NINE PUBLISHING CO., INC.
All Rights Reserved   Used by Permission

come   to take his chil - dren home. __

Verse

3. It's ____ the same sto - ry   the   crow told me, __ it's   the
4. I   live in   a   sil - ver mine __ and   I

on - ly one __ he knows.   Like   the morn - ing __ I
call   it Beg - gar's Tomb.   I   got __ me a

sun you come __ and __ like   the wind __ you go.
vi - o - lin ____ and I   beg you call __ the tune.

Ain't   no time __ to hate, ____   bare - ly time __ to wait. __
An - y - bod - y's choice, __   I   can hear __ your voice. __

____   Whoa,   oh, __ what I   want __ to know: _____
____   Whoa,   oh, __ what I   want __ to know:

where __ does __ the time go?
how __ does __ the song go?

Chorus

Come hear Un - cle John's Band by the riv - er - side. __
Come hear Un - cle John's Band play - ing to the tide. __

__ Got some things to talk ___ a - bout __
__ Come on a - long or go ___ a - lone, __ he's

1.
here be - side the __ ris - ing tide. __

2.
come to take his __ chil - - dren home.

Outro

Da da da da da da. Da da da da da

da. Da da da da da da.

Upside Down

from the Universal Pictures and Imagine Entertainment film CURIOUS GEORGE
Words and Music by Jack Johnson

Copyright © 2006 BUBBLE TOES PUBLISHING and UNIVERSAL PICTURES MUSIC
All Rights Controlled and Administered by UNIVERSAL MUSIC CORP.
All Rights Reserved   Used by Permission

Wild Horses

Words and Music by Mick Jagger and Keith Richards

© 1970 (Renewed) ABKCO MUSIC INC., 85 Fifth Avenue, New York, NY 10003
All Rights Reserved   Used by Permission

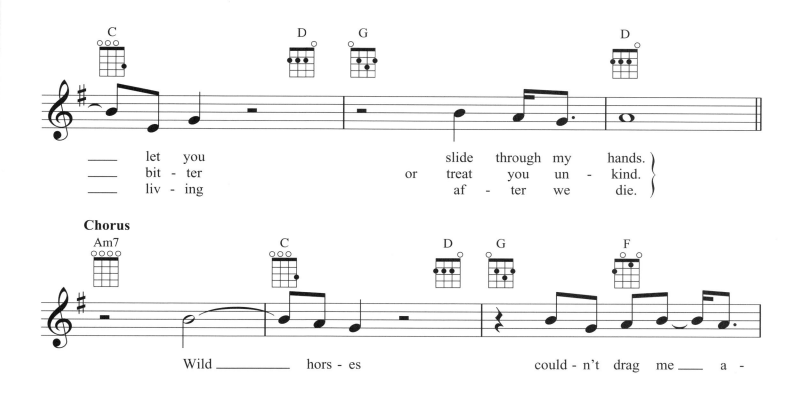

let you   slide through my   hands.
bit - ter   or   treat   you   un - kind.
liv - ing   af - ter   we   die.

Chorus

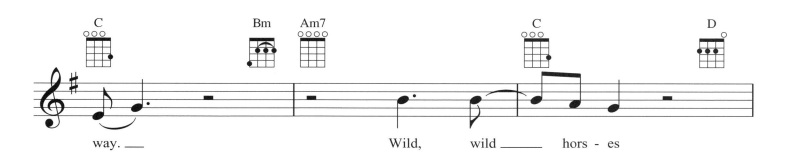

Wild _____ hors - es   could - n't drag me ___ a -

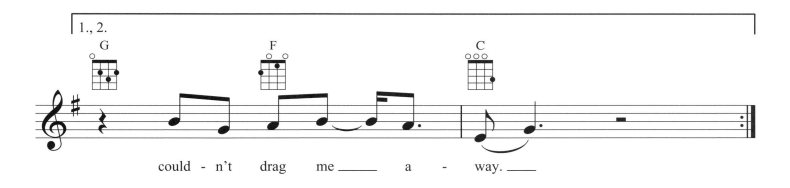

way. ___   Wild,   wild _____ hors - es

1., 2.

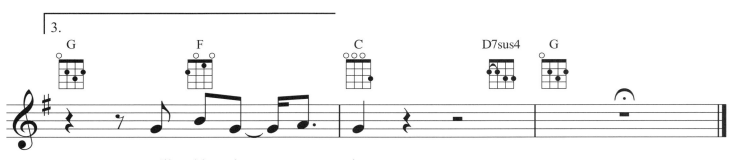

could - n't drag me _____ a - way. ___

3.

we'll ride them __ some - day.

167

You Belong with Me

Words and Music by Taylor Swift and Liz Rose

Copyright © 2008 Sony/ATV Music Publishing LLC, Taylor Swift Music, Potting Shed Music and Barbara Orbison World Publishing
All Rights on behalf of Sony/ATV Music Publishing LLC and Taylor Swift Music Administered by
Sony/ATV Music Publishing LLC, 424 Church Street, Suite 1200, Nashville, TN 37219
All Rights on behalf of Potting Shed Music and Barbara Orbison World Publishing Administered by BMG Rights Management (US) LLC
International Copyright Secured   All Rights Reserved

mu - sic she does - n't like, _____ and she'll nev - er
while since she brought you down. _____ You say you're fine; I know you

know your sto - ry like I do.
bet - ter than that. Hey, what - cha do - ing with a

Pre-Chorus

girl like that?
She wears wears short high skirts, heels,

But she wears short skirts,
She wears high heels,

I wear T - shirts, } she's cheer cap - tain and I'm on the bleach - ers,
I wear sneak - ers, }

dream - ing 'bout the day when you'll wake up and find _____ that what you're

look - ing for _____ has been here _____ the whole time. If you could

You be - long _ with me. _____

Bridge

Oh, I re - mem - ber you driv - ing to my house in the

mid - dle of the night. I'm the one who makes you laugh when you

know you're 'bout to cry. I know your fa - v'rite songs, and you

tell me 'bout your dreams. Think I know where you be - long. Think I

D.S. al Coda
(take 2nd ending)

Coda

know it's with me. _____ Can't you _____

The Wizard

Words and Music by Mark Clarke and Kenneth Hensley

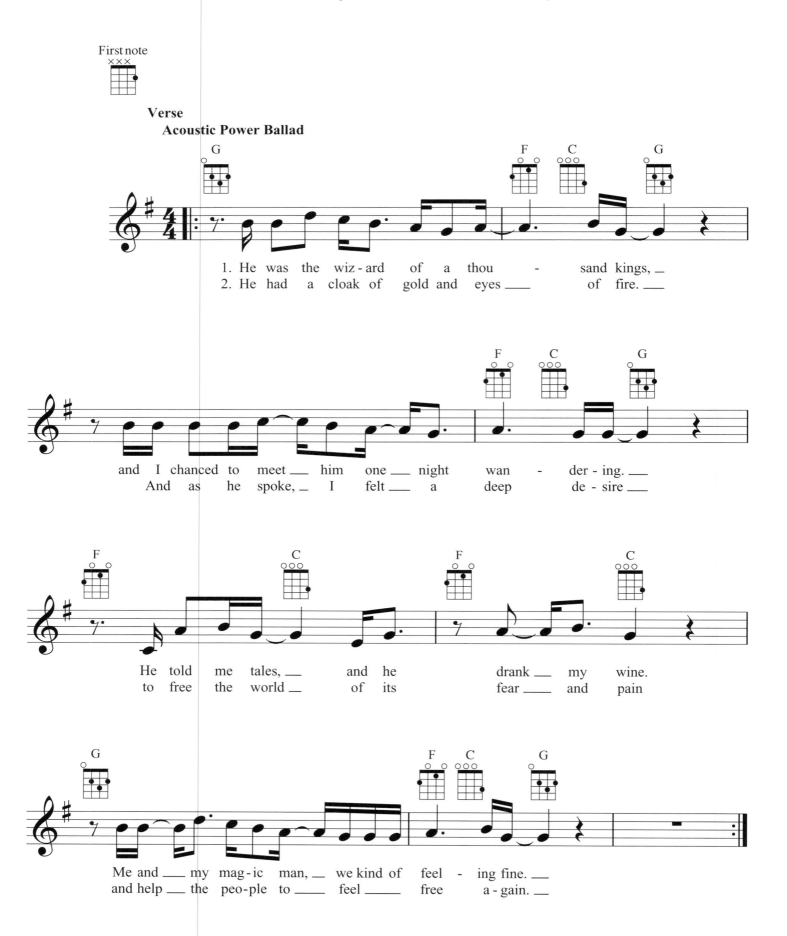

1. He was the wiz-ard of a thou - sand kings, __
2. He had a cloak of gold and eyes __ of fire. __

and I chanced to meet __ him one __ night wan - der - ing. __
And as he spoke, __ I felt __ a deep de - sire __

He told me tales, __ and he drank __ my wine.
to free the world __ of its fear __ and pain

Me and __ my mag-ic man, __ we kind of feel - ing fine. __
and help __ the peo-ple to __ feel __ free a - gain. __

© 1972 (Renewed 2000) EMI MUSIC PUBLISHING LTD.
All Rights in the U.S. and Canada Controlled and Administered by COLGEMS-EMI MUSIC INC.
All Rights Reserved   International Copyright Secured   Used by Permission

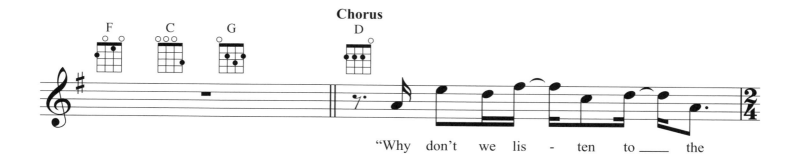

"Why don't we lis - ten to ____ the

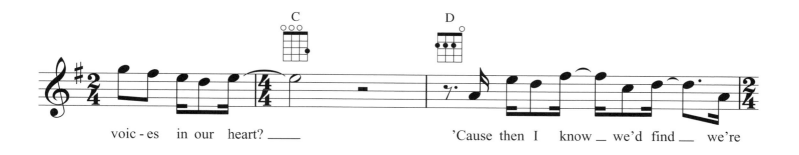

voic - es in our heart? ____ 'Cause then I know ___ we'd find ___ we're

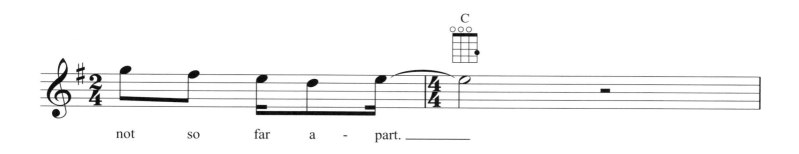

not so far a - part. _____

Ev - 'ry - bod - y's got ___ to be hap - py, ev - 'ry - one should sing. ___

____ For we know the joy ___ of life, ___ the

173

peace that love can bring." ____   3. So spoke the wiz - ard   in his

moun - tain home. ___   The vi - sion of his wis - dom means ___ we'll

nev - er be a - lone. ___   And I will dream ___ of my

mag - ic night, ___   and the mil - lion sil - ver stars ___ that

guide me with their light. ___